The authors would like to thank Tim for his help, patience and support.
In addition: all at Mr Christian's Delicatessen for their help with ingredients;
'the boys' at Oddbins and at Corney & Barrow, Kensington Park Road, London,
for their help with the drinks suggestions; Colin MacIvor.

This book is for all friends who realize the importance of buying
good produce for fast cooking.

The publisher would like to thank Formica Ltd.

The right of Marie-Pierre Moine, Henrietta Green and Lewis Esson to be identified
as Authors of this Work has been asserted by them in accordance with the
Copyright, Designs and Patents Act 1988.

First published in 1996 by
Conran Octopus Limited, 37 Shelton Street,
London WC2H 9HN

Reprinted 1997

Text copyright
© Lewis Esson, Henrietta Green
and Marie-Pierre Moine 1996
Design and layout copyright
© Conran Octopus Limited 1996

All rights reserved. No part of this book may be
reproduced, stored in a retrieval system or
transmitted in any form or by any means,
electronic, electrostatic, magnetic tape,
mechanical, photocopying or otherwise, without
prior permission in writing of the publisher.

British Library Cataloguing in Publication Data.
ISBN 1-85029-728-2

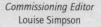

Commissioning Editor
Louise Simpson

Project Editor
Charlotte Coleman-Smith

Assistant Editor
Tessa Clayton

Art Director
Helen Lewis

Designers
Town Group Consultancy and
Liz Hallam

Copy Editor
Penny David

Home Economist
Meg Jansz

Stylist
Nato Welton

Production
Julia Golding

Calligrapher
Andrew Whiteley

Index
Helen Baz

Printed and bound by
KHL Printing, Singapore

fast food for friends

Lewis Esson

with

Henrietta Green &

Marie-Pierre Moine

photography by

Patrice de Villiers

CONRAN OCTOPUS

BRUNCHES AND LUNCHES

CASUAL MEALS

FINGER AND FORK FOOD

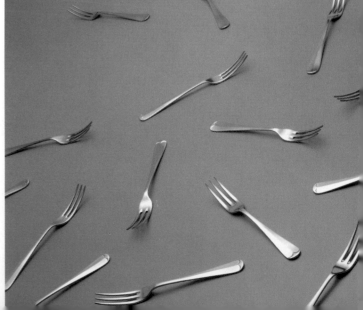

DINNER PARTIES

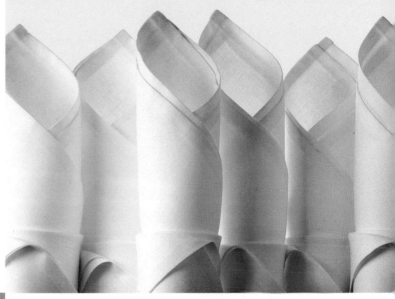

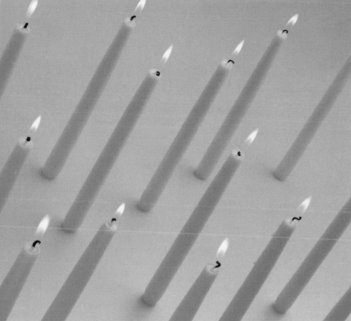

SPECIAL OCCASIONS

TREASURY OF BASIC RECIPES TO IMPRESS WITHOUT EFFORT

Introduction

INTRODUCTION

More than anything else, 'having friends over' for a meal - whatever the occasion - should be fun for all concerned. For this reason, this book tries to avoid rules but instead supplies lots of well-tried and well-loved combinations as well as giving as much advice on preparation and timing as is practical. However, first take the time to read through the following notes on menu planning, time management, shopping, equipment and ingredients. Being just that little bit prepared before you start cooking – especially by having a well-stocked store-cupboard – will make all the difference, not only to how fast you can get food on the table but to how much you and your guests will enjoy the experience.

MENU PLANNING

Fast Food For Friends consists of a series of set menus; however, we know well enough how we use our own favourite cookbooks to realize that readers don't necessarily stick to menu suggestions verbatim, so there follow a few simple guidelines on the subject.

Think of a meal as a symphony or a good story with a beginning, a middle and an end, different movements and changes of pace. Try to present a good range of tastes and textures — if you start with a rich, creamy dish, avoid creamy puddings and (with the exception of olive oil and other basics) avoid using the same ingredients prominently twice if you can — although a garlicky first course and a touch of garlic later on is fine as is, say, a citrusy dessert after a hint of lemon or lime in an earlier dish.

When you plan the meal, try to imagine what it will feel like to look at it and eat it, course by course. Notice any potential gaps. If, for example, you have a very light starter and pudding, include some nice stodge like rice or pasta with the main course, or buy some good bread and a splendid cheese to finish. Try not to overload your guests with calories, fats or animal protein, but never be too sparing with portions — unless that's what your guests want (see Low-fat Lunch on page 24 for ideas for entertaining dieters).

Colour and presentation — eye appeal in general — are almost as important as flavour. Try to arrange variations on a theme or some pleasant contrasts. Fiddly garnishes and 'pictures on plates' are certainly not in the spirit of *Fast Food For Friends*, although a few snipped herbs or a dusting of paprika over a very monochromatic dish can make all the difference to its visual impact.

Even when not particularly pressed for time it is wise to try to incorporate into the menu at least one dish which may be fully prepared ahead of time, like a chilled soup which can sit in the fridge until last-minute garnishing, a simple ice cream with a sauce, or a flavoured cream over fresh fruit for dessert. This not only speeds things up during the course of the meal; it also allows the cook more of a chance to enjoy the guests' company.

The Perfect Party-giver's Pantry

It is amazing how many unexpected situations you can take in your stride if your kitchen is well stocked. Obviously you don't need to have all of the following all of the time, but none of it will go to waste and as well as allowing you to entertain effortlessly it will also pep up your everyday cooking and ring more changes in family meals.

The secret is to use always the best possible ingredients; for example, best-quality extra virgin olive oil for salad dressings and for cooking, and sea salt and freshly ground black pepper rather than the processed varieties. Add fresh herbs, where possible, rather than dried.

In the larder:

loaf of good bread
half a dozen eggs
1 or 2 heads of garlic
packet of sea salt
packet of black peppercorns
4 or 5 red onions
4 or 5 lemons
3 or 4 limes
2 or 3 oranges

On the windowsill:

small pots of fresh herbs, especially:
  chives
  flat-leaf parsley
  basil
  dill

In the refrigerator:

575ml/1pt milk
225g/8oz unsalted butter
225g/8oz unsmoked streaky bacon
300ml/^{1}/2pt plain runny yogurt
300ml/^{1}/2pt crème fraîche, double
  cream or fromage frais

TIME MANAGEMENT

The aim of this book is to enable you to produce delicious meals as quickly and painlessly as possible. Some people prefer a very sharp burst of intense activity; they are the sprinters of the kitchen. Others prefer a more relaxed approach and are happier spending a little longer, perhaps breaking up their efforts to have a chat on the phone or a drink with their guests — think of them as culinary ramblers.

Fast Food For Friends mixes the two approaches: Sunday Lunch, for example (see page 19), takes longer to cook but needs little preparation and last-minute effort, while the Congratulations Party (see page 124) requires a short but concentrated attention span. The Fast Flow box exists as a guideline to help you plan and see at a glance how the menu can best be handled. No precise timings are given since they tend to make some people waste time nervously watching the clock. Once you have decided on a menu, take some precious time to read the recipes and glance at the suggested Fast Flow. The main thing here is to know yourself as a cook. If you don't enjoy cooking in public, work out where and when you can have breaks while you prepare the meal – none of the recipes in *Fast Food For Friends* are a succession of uninterrupted *moments critiques*. If you like everything organized to the last detail, make sure you leave nothing to chance (there is always an element of unpredictability in the kitchen). If you enjoy cooking with others and employing your guests as *sous chefs*, work out in advance what you'll get them to do.

Make sure you have all the ingredients, utensils and equipment you need. Put them within reach. Chill drinks that need to be chilled, lay the table and prepare the aperitif tray. Then take a deep breath, grab a glass of something to drink and start cooking. Never forget that it should be fun and that guests who have enjoyed two aperitifs will enjoy themselves more with a relaxed host than if they had sat down ten minutes earlier with a flustered wreck.

SHOPPING ON THE WAY HOME

It was that great food writer, the late Jane Grigson, who wrote that good cooking is all about shopping. To cook well, you must have good ingredients, to cook fast you should add certain convenience foods to the list. This means pre-washed and cut vegetables, pre-packed and selected salad leaves, packets of trimmed herbs, meat that is trimmed, butchered and, if necessary, boned, and fish that is skinned and filleted. You will be amazed at the time it will save you.

It is vital to be organized, particularly if you intend to follow the meals as set out in this book. List all the ingredients you require and buy the fresh ones on or as near to the day you intend to cook them as possible, so they remain in peak condition. If you work and your workplace has a refrigerator with space for your shopping, so much the better; you can shop on your way into work or at lunch time. Otherwise stop off on your way home, as most supermarkets now stay open late.

Try to keep your larder well stocked – the vital ingredients that every fast cook should have are listed here – replacing items when you run out. Remember that sound shopping is the first step to easy fast cooking.

large chunk of Parmesan cheese
225g/8oz Cheddar cheese
packet of ready-washed salad leaves
bunch of spring onions
head of radicchio
2 or 3 red or yellow peppers
1 or 2 chilli peppers
450g/1lb tasty tomatoes
jar of good ready-made mustard
bottle of dry white wine
1/2 bottle of dry sherry

In the freezer:
another loaf of good bread
another 225g/8oz unsalted butter
packet of muffins and/or potato
   pancakes and/or blinis
225g/8oz leaf spinach
115g/4oz small garden peas
1 litre/1 3/4pt good vanilla ice cream
1.1 litres /2pt chicken stock
ice cubes

In the store-cupboard:
450g/1lb basmati rice
450g/1lb pasta
450g/1lb easy-cook Oriental noodles
packet of court-bouillon
bottle of extra virgin olive oil
bottle of olive oil (for cooking)
bottle of sunflower oil
small can or bottle of walnut oil
small bottle of chilli oil
small bottle of dark sesame oil
bottle of red or white wine vinegar or
   cider vinegar
small bottle of sherry vinegar
small bottle of balsamic vinegar
bottle of good-quality soy sauce
tin of English mustard powder
tin of five-spice powder
large jar of good-quality mayonnaise
   (keep in refrigerator once opened)

tube or bottle of anchovy essence (keep
    in refrigerator once opened)
tube of tomato paste (keep in
    refrigerator once opened)
large bottle of Worcestershire sauce
bottle of Tabasco sauce
bottle of harissa or chilli sauce
packet of whole nutmegs
drum of paprika
packet of cumin seeds
packet of oregano
packet of small dried chillies
packet of dried wild mushrooms
jar of sun-dried tomatoes in oil
jar of capers
packet of soft brown sugar
packet of icing sugar
jar of clear honey
jar of redcurrant jelly
jar of good marmalade
large bar of good-quality dark
    chocolate
packet of blanched almonds
packet of seedless raisins
packet of pine nuts
packet of walnut halves
packet of hazelnuts
packet of poppy seeds
packet of sesame seeds
jar of tahini (sesame seed paste)

In cans:
clams in brine
tuna fish in oil
anchovy fillets in salt or oil
good-quality sardines
artichoke hearts
cannellini beans
chickpeas
flageolets
sweetcorn kernels
red sweet peppers
chopped tomatoes (several cans)

EQUIPMENT

Apart from a few good sharp knives and a set of sturdy saucepans (preferably with tight-fitting lids) little specialist equipment is required to cook the food in this book. However, the following items are useful:

Food processor It is fairly obvious that these speed up chopping and mixing in any situation. However, you will see that we often shred vegetables, like potatoes, for speedier cooking and the food processor does this perfectly. It is also almost magical when used to make sauces like mayonnaise (see page 138). Try to get one of the new machines with a detachable small bowl for small amounts. If you can manage to give your food processor permanent space on a work top, you will save time and you will use it more readily.

Scissors Have a couple of good pairs of all-purpose kitchen scissors and keep them sharp. They are useful for everything from jointing poultry to snipping herbs.

Zester A lemon zester allows you to pare off strips of peel from citrus fruit without lifting off any of the bitter pith.

Salad spinner A salad spinner gets leaves really dry and saves time.

Pastry brush A good stout pastry or paint brush is useful for applying oil to food, grill racks, ridged grilling pans and so on, but avoid nylon bristles as they may melt on contact with hot items.

Wok A wok is essential for stir-frying. Buy one with a matching scoop to stir the food. The single-handled versions are easier to manœuvre. Buy the very basic and inexpensive ones from Chinese supermarkets and replace them when you need to.

Pasta pan A proper tall pasta pan with an inner basket so that the pasta may be lifted from the water with ease is expensive, but worth paying a little extra for.

Ridged grilling pan These heat quickly and seal and cook steaks, chops, small whole fish etc. in minutes (you need a gas hob). They also give the feeling of barbecued food without hours of fiddling with charcoal and a chance to get the decorative effect of *quadrillage* (seared crosshatching, see pages 102 and 117) on your meats.

Sauté pan A good-quality sauté pan is worth the investment. Make sure the base is thick and heavy for even browning and that the sides are quite high so that the food can be stirred vigorously and liquid ingredients added later. It should also come with a tight-fitting lid for subsequent slower cooking after the initial browning.

Frying pans Try to have one or two frying pans in different sizes to match the type and quantity of food being cooked. Non-stick pans are best as they permit healthy dry-frying. A small omelette pan is also very useful.

TECHNIQUES

Snipping Snip herbs and leaves with scissors directly into pans or salad bowls rather than chopping them on boards. Firm fruit and food such as chicken livers, mushrooms and sliced cooked meats can also be snipped. A quick way of cutting salad and herb leaves into shreds is to pile them on top of each other, roll them up tightly and then snip the roll across with scissors (this is called a *chiffonnade*).

Tearing and shredding Tear or shred food like salad leaves or cooked chicken into bowls or pans. It is not only quicker than chopping but gives ingredients a better texture and helps retain more of their juices.

Crumbling and flaking Wherever possible, crumble and flake foods like cheese and cooked fish into pans and bowls rather than taking the time (and the utensils) to chop them.

Grating Many foods, including firmer vegetables as well as cheese, can be grated instead of being finely chopped. For larger quantities of ingredients, use a food processor.

Whizzing The phrase 'whizz in the food processor' that we use in the recipes means to process just long enough to achieve the desired texture. It is usually necessary to break the food into manageable pieces first so the machine can deal with them efficiently. When whizzing, be careful not to over-process foods, as they can easily become a textureless mush.

Zesting The recipes in *Fast Food For Friends* make a great deal of use of the zest of citrus fruits. Use only uncoated fruit or fruit that has been well scrubbed in warm soapy water then rinsed and dried. Grate the zest with the fine section of a grater (if you stretch some clingfilm over the grater first, it will remain intact and come off with all the residual zest still clinging to it) or pare it with a zester. Either way, try not to press too hard so as not to bring up too much of the bitter pith that lies underneath the peel.

Using garlic A quick and easy means of flavouring with garlic is to halve a clove and rub it over the bottom of a pan or bowl, or smear it directly over firm food. Otherwise, crush garlic cloves with the side of a wide knife or use a garlic press.

Heating water For dishes that require boiling water, heating the water in a kettle will really speed things up. For dishes like pasta, rice and soups when a large amount of water is called for, heat some in the kettle and the rest in a saucepan.

Grilling When grilling, turn on the grill as early as possible so that it has time to get properly heated while you are preparing the ingredients. Try to use uniformly thin pieces of food for quick and even cooking.

Pan-grilling The secret with pan-grilling is to get the ridged grill pan good and hot over the gas hob before you start cooking. Place the food carefully on it and leave undisturbed until the surface in contact is well cooked (you can always test by edging up a little corner). Turn the food over carefully and repeat with the other side. (See pages 102 and 117 for how to obtain *quadrillage*, the neat cross-hatched searing on the surface of the food.) If the food being pan-grilled does not have much natural fat, then grease the pan well first with oil, preferably an oil such as groundnut, which takes high temperatures well.

Sautéing In this very useful technique, the main ingredients — usually cut into small pieces — are initially cooked in butter or oil with frequent stirring over a high heat to brown and seal them. Flavourings, such as wine and herbs, are then added to the pan and the dish is simmered gently for a few minutes more to finish the cooking process.

Stir-frying This is similar to sautéing but is done in a wok. The food is usually cut into strips or small pieces and is kept on the move all the time over quite a high heat. The curved shape of the wok allows cooked food to be moved to the cooler rim while newly added ingredients are cooked in the hotter base.

Deglazing After food has been pan-fried or grilled, the pan is usually deglazed with a little liquid, such as water, stock, vinegar, lemon juice, wine or other alcohol. Stirring the liquid over the heat with a wooden spoon and scraping up the sediment gets all the flavour from the base of the pan to make a good sauce or gravy.

Brunches and lunches

THE ROLLING WEEKEND BREAKFAST

- BACON AND MUSHROOM KEDGEREE
- SMOKED FISH AND TOMATO FRITTATA
- POTATO PANCAKES WITH SPICED APPLE SAUCE

FAST-PREPARED SUNDAY LUNCH

- MOZZARELLA CROSTINI
- BAKED LAMB SHANKS
- ROASTED NEW POTATOES
- GREEN BEANS AND BROCCOLI WITH PARSLEY AND WALNUTS
- CHOCOLATE AND CAMPARI SOUFFLÉED PUDDINGS

LOW-FAT LUNCH

- AUBERGINE DIP
- CHINESE-STYLE SOUP
- FRUIT SLICES WITH FRESH MINT

THE WORKING LUNCH

- BULLION BOUILLON IN A MUG WITH PARMESAN CRISPS
- BIG-DEAL PIZZA
- ASSORTED SWEETENERS

THE ROLLING WEEKEND BREAKFAST

This is a meal for languorous Sunday mornings when friends drift in – or get up – to eat at different times. None of the dishes will suffer if kept warm or left to go cold; in fact, some will even improve or take on different characteristics.

The neat twist to this menu is breaking up the two traditional breakfast pairings of bacon and eggs and smoked fish with rice and realigning them to greater effect. Some freshly baked buttered rolls or *petits pains* (try the supermarket part-baked ones) and an assortment of good-quality jams and marmalades will round off this feast beautifully.

BACON AND
MUSHROOM KEDGEREE

SMOKED FISH AND
TOMATO FRITTATA

POTATO PANCAKES
WITH SPICED
APPLE SAUCE

FOR 6–8

BACON AND MUSHROOM KEDGEREE

In England, kedgeree has become associated with smoked fish. However, the original Indian dish used pulses like split peas or lentils, so feel free to experiment with any ingredients you wish. For vegetarians, omit the bacon.

6 cardamom pods
225g/8oz basmati rice
6 rashers of smoked back bacon
2 red onions
30g/1oz butter
225g/8oz mushrooms, preferably organic brown-cap
1 lime
handful of parsley
handful of coriander
150ml/¹/₄pt crème fraîche
pinch of ground cumin
pinch or two of cayenne
salt and pepper
lime wedges, to serve

1 Put a large pan of lightly salted water on to boil. Lightly crush the cardamom pods and add to the water. Put the rice in a sieve and rinse it under the cold tap, then tip into the pan and bring to the boil. Stir, cover and cook for about 10 minutes, until just *al dente*.

2 Meanwhile, cut the bacon into strips and dry-fry until crisp and lightly browned. Remove from the pan and keep warm. Cut the onions into chunks and fry in the bacon fat until just soft.

3 At the same time, melt the butter in another frying pan over a moderate to high heat. Wipe then quarter the mushrooms. Sauté until just softened.

4 When the rice is ready, drain, then return it to the pan and remove the cardamom pieces. Place the rice over a very low heat and fluff it with a fork.

5 Grate in the lime zest, then squeeze in the juice. Snip in the fresh herbs, reserving a little of each for garnish. Add the onions, bacon, mushrooms and the crème fraîche with the cumin. Stir well over a moderate heat to warm through. Season to taste with salt, pepper and cayenne, and garnish with lime wedges and the reserved herbs.

TO DRINK

Pots of strong breakfast tea and freshly brewed coffee – what goes better with smoked fish and bacon, after all? For those for whom a party is not a party without alcohol, however, make up a pitcher of sparkling white wine mixed with fruit nectar like peach or guava, perhaps fortified with a fruit brandy if you think your guests may need a hair-of-the-dog.

FAST FLOW

1 Preheat oven if cooking or warming rolls

2 Put on kettle of water for tomatoes

3 Prepare apples and start cooking sauce

4 Poach fish

5 Blanch and peel tomatoes

6 Rinse rice and start to cook

7 Cook bacon, onions and mushrooms

8 Drain rice and dry off

9 Add flavourings and other ingredients to rice and heat through

10 Prepare potatoes for pancakes

11 Start cooking pancakes

12 Prepare mix for frittata

13 Cook frittata in pan

14 Finish frittata under grill

15 Finish apple sauce

SMOKED FISH AND TOMATO FRITTATA

This tasty and filling egg cake combines two of the favourite flavour combinations of childhood – the chopped egg and tomato sandwich filling and smoked haddock and eggs poached in milk. The perfect brunch dish, this is just as good piping hot as it is warm or cool; it also reheats well if done carefully. It tastes quite different with each mouthful as various flavours come to the fore or combine differently.

about 450g/1lb undyed smoked haddock
about 150ml/¹/₄pt milk
1–2 bay leaves
4–5 black peppercorns
450g/1lb plum tomatoes
handful of flat-leaf parsley
handful of dill fronds
bunch of chives
6 eggs
3 tbsp crème fraîche
dash or two of Worcestershire sauce
2–4 drops of Tabasco sauce, to taste
1 tsp horseradish sauce
30g/1oz Parmesan cheese
20g/¹/₂oz butter
salt and pepper

1 Put a kettle of water on to heat. Rinse the haddock under cold running water and put in a pan with just enough milk to cover (cut the fish into manageable pieces if necessary). Add a bay leaf or two and some black peppercorns, bring to the boil and poach gently for 2–4 minutes, until the fish is stiff and beginning to flake (the exact time will depend on how thick it is). Drain and leave to cool.

2 Meanwhile, put the tomatoes in a heatproof bowl and pour over boiling water from the kettle. Leave for a minute and then pour off the water. The skins should now peel off readily. Remove the stalk ends and cut each tomato into eight wedges. Reserve the wedges in a bowl.

3 When the fish is cool enough to handle, flake into the bowl of tomatoes, taking care to remove any bones.

4 Rinse the herbs and snip half of each into the bowl of fish and tomatoes. Season with pepper and mix lightly.

5 Break the eggs into another bowl and beat until frothy. Season and stir in the crème fraîche. Add the Worcestershire sauce, Tabasco and horseradish sauce. Snip in the remaining herbs. Mix well.

6 Preheat the grill to high and grate the Parmesan. Melt the butter in a frying pan with a heatproof handle over a moderate heat, tilting it to make sure the sides as well as the base are well coated. Increase the heat to high.

7 As soon as the butter starts to smoke, stir the egg mixture well again and tip it into the pan. With a spatula, quickly lift the solidifying egg away from the edges and into the centre of the pan to distribute it evenly, then tip the fish and tomato mixture on top. Spread it out evenly with a fork and continue to cook over a slightly reduced heat for about 3 minutes, until the base is firmly set.

8 Sprinkle over the cheese and put the frittata under the grill as close to the heat as possible. Grill until the top is set. Serve cut into wedges.

Bacon and Mushroom Kedgeree (see page 15)

GREEN BEANS AND BROCCOLI WITH PARSLEY AND WALNUTS

about 350g/12oz fine green beans
about 350g/12oz small broccoli florets
2 tbsp fruity olive oil
55g/2oz fresh walnut kernels
several sprigs of flat-leaf parsley
2 tsp lemon juice
salt and pepper

1 Boil a kettle of water. Pour into a pan, season with salt, place over a high heat and return to a fast boil.

2 Top and tail the beans. Tip them into the boiling water, return to the boil and cook vigorously for 2–3 minutes.

3 Tip in the broccoli, bring back to the boil and cook for 3–4 minutes, or until cooked to taste. Drain.

4 Arrange the drained vegetables attractively on a serving platter. Drizzle over half the olive oil, then sprinkle over the walnut kernels. Snip over several parsley leaves and toss very lightly.

5 If necessary, adjust the seasoning. Drizzle over the rest of the olive oil and the lemon juice. Serve the vegetables as soon as possible with the lamb and roasted potatoes.

CHOCOLATE AND CAMPARI SOUFFLÉED PUDDINGS

A cross between a pudding and a soufflé, this dessert tastes of dark chocolate, bitters and orange and has a pleasing, gooey inside texture.

170g/6oz dark bitter chocolate
2 tbsp Campari
1 orange
unsalted butter, for greasing
2 tbsp crème fraîche, plus extra to serve (optional)
3 very fresh large eggs, separated
75g/2¹/₂oz caster sugar
icing sugar, for dusting (optional)
extra orange zest, to serve (optional)

1 Preheat the oven to 190°C/375°F/gas 5. Break the chocolate into pieces. Put in a pan with a tablespoon of water and stir over a very low heat until melted. Stir in the Campari and grate in the orange zest. If you are not ready to bake the puddings, stand the pan over very hot water and stir occasionally.

2 Grease with butter four or five 10cm/4in soufflé dishes or ramekins.

3 Take the saucepan off the heat and, using a whisk, work the cream into the melted chocolate. Stir in the egg yolks.

4 In a bowl, whisk the egg whites. When they stiffen, lightly whisk in the sugar. Using a large metal spoon, carefully fold the whisked egg whites into the chocolate cream.

5 Spoon the mixture into the buttered dishes. Bake for about 20 minutes, until well risen and a little crusty on the outside but still soft and moist inside (prod gently to test).

6 Dust the puddings lightly with icing sugar and sprinkle over the orange zest, if using. Serve immediately.

Baked Lamb Shanks (see page 21)

CHINESE-STYLE SOUP

A good fish stock makes all the difference to this soup. You can sometimes buy it in pots from the supermarket, but failing that, use a vegetable rather than a fish stock cube as the flavour is far less obtrusive.

1 litre/1³/₄pt fish stock (see above)
2 garlic cloves
2.5cm/1in piece of fresh ginger
2.5cm/1in piece of fresh lemon grass
3 spring onions
225g/8oz fresh and meaty white fish fillets, such as cod or hake
2 medium squid
¹/₂ head of Chinese cabbage or 1 cos lettuce
115g/4oz oyster mushrooms
115g/4oz baby sweetcorn
1 tbsp chilli oil
115g/4oz rice thread noodles
1 tbsp soy sauce
85g/3oz peeled prawns
1 tbsp dry sherry (optional)
large bunch of coriander
salt and pepper

1   Heat the stock in a saucepan until it reaches boiling point.

2   Meanwhile, whizz the garlic, ginger, lemon grass and spring onions to a paste in a food processor.

3   Skin the fish and cut into strips. Cut the squid into rings about 2.5cm/1in wide and cut the tentacles in half. Shred the Chinese cabbage, chop the mushrooms and cut the sweetcorn in half lengthwise.

4   Heat the oil in a wok or cast-iron casserole until hot, then add the paste and stir-fry for about 1 minute.

5   Add the fish strips and stir-fry them for a further minute.

6   Add the Chinese cabbage, mushrooms and sweetcorn and stir-fry for a further minute.

7   Ladle the boiling stock into the wok, break in the thread noodles and stir to separate. Add the soy sauce and simmer for a few minutes until the noodles are almost soft.

8   Stir in the squid rings and prawns and simmer for about 1 minute to heat through. The squid cooks very quickly; you will be able to tell that it is done when it turns opaque.

9   Just before serving, stir in the sherry (if using), snip over the coriander leaves and adjust the seasoning. Ladle into individual soup bowls and serve.

FRUIT SLICES WITH FRESH MINT

As a general rule of thumb, allow about 55–85g/2–3oz fruit per person. For really fast work, choose fruit that does not need peeling, such as plums, strawberries, apricots, figs, apples, pears or any of the summer berries.

fresh fruit (see above)
¹/₂ lemon
small bunch of mint
2 tbsp sweet white wine

1   Cut the larger fruit into thin slices and arrange all the fruit attractively on a large plate. Squeeze the lemon juice over the fruit to prevent it discolouring.

2   Chop the mint and scatter it over the fruit. Finally, sprinkle over the white wine. Place the plate in the fridge until ready to serve.

Chinese-style Soup

Big-deal Pizza

The idea of fried pizza comes from Elizabeth David's seminal *Italian Food* and has great potential for the fast cook. The dough is very quick to make – no resting or proving is required – and it puffs up to a particularly delicious crisp crust in the frying pan. You put the toppings on as the second side is frying and cover with a tight-fitting lid (you do need a large frying pan – at least 25cm/10in diameter) to give an instant oven effect. In 10 minutes your pizza is cooked to perfection.

1 small red onion

8 thin slices of prosciutto

200g/7oz Mozzarella cheese

**170g/6oz flour, plus extra for
   dusting**

2 heaped tsp baking powder

2 heaped tsp dried oregano

olive oil, for frying

225g/8oz passata

6–8 anchovies in oil, drained

1 tbsp small capers, drained

handful of basil leaves

2 tbsp stoned black olives

salt and pepper

1   Dice the onion or cut it into thick slices, tear the prosciutto into strips and cut the Mozzarella into slices. Set aside.

2   Sift the flour into a large mixing bowl with the baking powder. Mix in a generous pinch of salt and half the oregano. Create a well in the middle and pour into it about 100ml/3$\frac{1}{2}$fl oz of cold water. With your fingers, gradually mix in the flour from the edges to make a smooth dough. You may need to adjust the consistency with a little more water or flour to get a smooth elastic dough that does not stick to the fingers. Knead well for a minute or so on a floured surface.

3   Coat the bottom of a large heavy frying pan (see above) with olive oil and put over a moderate to high heat.

4   Roll the dough out to a thin round big enough to fit the bottom of the pan.

5   When the oil is just on the point of smoking, but not quite, lift the dough wrapped around the rolling pin and drop it carefully into the hot oil. You may have to rearrange it with a fork to fit flat in the pan. Fry briskly for a few minutes until the base is a good golden colour. With a fork, prick any air bubbles that rise and flatten them back down.

6   Turn the dough over and reduce the heat to moderate. Spread the passata over the cooked top of the pizza. Season generously and sprinkle with the remaining oregano. Arrange the onions slices over the top. Next, add the anchovy strips and scatter over the capers. Arrange the cheese slices on top. Tuck the prosciutto strips here and there. Finish by tearing the basil leaves and strewing them and the olives over the top.

7   Cover the pan and cook until the base is golden and the cheese has melted. Lift out carefully using two spatulas and drain on paper towels. Serve cut into wedges.

Variation

Make the dough with sugar instead of salt, spread it with a good-quality apricot jam and top with a fruit compôte to make a delicious and unusual dessert.

Casual meals

LOW-COST DINNER FOR LARGE NUMBERS

- VITE-YSSOISE
- QUICK COUSCOUS
- APPLE AND GINGER CRUNCH MERINGUE

UNEXPECTED GUESTS

- RISOTTO DELLA CASA
- SCALLOPINE WITH ORANGE AND MARSALA
- CARROTS, BROAD BEANS AND MANGETOUT WITH THYME
- RASPBERRY AND MERINGUE CREAM

VEGETARIAN SUPPER

- CHICORY WITH BLUE CHEESE AND WALNUTS
- ROAST OYSTER MUSHROOMS WITH TAGLIATELLE
- SALAD WITH PINK GRAPEFRUIT DRESSING
- BRIOCHE SPLITS

THE FATTED CALF

- QUICK CLAM CHOWDER
- INDIVIDUAL BEEF WELLINGTONS WITH A MUSTARD SAUCE
- STIR-FRIED BRUSSELS SPROUTS WITH TOASTED PINE NUTS
- TRIFLE DELUXE

HOT AND SPICY FEAST

- QUICK PRAWN TOASTS
- PORK MEDALLIONS WITH GINGER AND ORANGE
- STIR-FRIED MIXED LEAVES
- CHILLI NOODLES
- CHILLED LYCHEE AND WALNUT CREAM

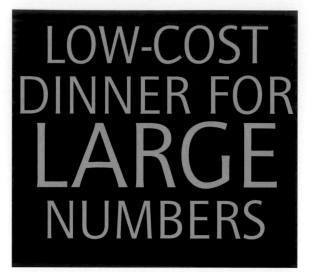

LOW-COST DINNER FOR LARGE NUMBERS

All too often nowadays feeding a crowd of friends unexpectedly means a flying visit to the chill counter of the nearest supermarket, but we all know how expensive that can be. Especially since those ready-meal packets that confidently say 'serves 4' usually only really manage to satisfy half that number. However, with just a little thought and imagination and a few staples from the store-cupboard you can produce a home-cooked meal with lots of character, without spending any more than you might on a predictable convenience banquet for four.

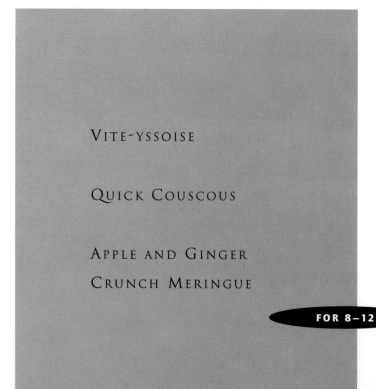

VITE-YSSOISE

QUICK COUSCOUS

APPLE AND GINGER
CRUNCH MERINGUE

FOR 8–12

VITE-YSSOISE

Served in a large tureen, a creamy vichysoisse soup completely belies its inexpensive origins. You can use canned consommé instead of stock in this recipe, or even a couple of the better (low-salt) stock cubes.

30g/1oz butter
1.1 litres/2pt good-quality chicken or vegetable stock
generous measure of white wine (optional)
450g/1lb thin leeks
2 celery stalks
450g/1lb floury potatoes
generous pinch of freshly ground mace or grated nutmeg
200ml/7fl oz crème fraîche (optional)
1 egg yolk
salt and pepper
chopped chives, chervil or tarragon, to garnish (optional)

1 Melt the butter in a large heavy-based pan over a low heat. Put the stock and the wine, if using, to heat in a separate pan.

2 Trim and rinse the leeks and celery and slice them thinly. Add to the butter and sauté gently for a few minutes until soft but not coloured.

3 While the leeks and celery are softening, peel the potatoes and dice as finely as possible. Add to the pan with some salt and pepper and a little mace or nutmeg. Stir to coat.

4 Add the boiling stock, bring to the boil and simmer for about 15 minutes, until the vegetables are just tender. Remove from the heat to cool slightly.

5 Either whizz in the blender or pass through a food mill to achieve a creamy texture that is not too smooth.

6 If using crème fraîche, put two-thirds of it into a bowl and mix in the egg yolk. Stir into the soup (off the heat) just before serving. If not using crème fraîche, mix the egg yolk into a few spoonfuls of the soup and return to the pan. Mix well and adjust the seasoning.

7 Serve topped with the remaining crème fraîche and the herbs, if using.

TO DRINK

A young dry white wine such as a Sauvignon with the soup, then a Moroccan gris or any dry rosé with the couscous. Or just drink what your guests bring in order of descending quality.

FAST FLOW

1
Warm soup stock; sauté vegetables

2
Heat water for couscous

3
Preheat oven for pudding and prepare dish

4
Put milk to heat

5
Prepare potatoes for soup, put in pan with stock; bring to simmer

6
Remove milk mixture from heat and grate in apples

7
Brown chicken and lamb; put in casserole, add boiling water, vegetables and flavourings

8
Skim stock

9
Add egg yolks to milk, pour into dish and put to bake

10
Add remaining vegetables and flavourings to casserole

11
Blend soup; add egg and cream. Pour boiling water over couscous

12
Remove custard from oven; prepare biscuits and whisk egg whites

13
Serve soup

14
Finish pudding and return to oven. Finish couscous and serve

Quick Couscous

This is a wonderfully filling dish. The ingredients are easy to come by, inexpensive and straightforward to cook, especially with today's packs of precooked couscous. However, delicate spicing and hot harissa seasoning transform this humble stew into a feast redolent of far-off romantic places.

3 tbsp oil, plus extra if necessary

8–12 chicken portions (thighs and drumsticks)

450g/1lb lean lamb

4 onions

6 garlic cloves

4 turnips

4 large carrots

good pinch of saffron strands

1 tsp each ground cumin, ginger and turmeric

2 good-quality low-salt chicken or vegetable stock cubes (or 1 of each)

6 large ripe tomatoes

8 courgettes

140g/5oz seedless raisins

bunch of flat-leaf parsley

bunch of coriander

400g/14oz canned cooked chickpeas, drained

675g/1¹/₂lb precooked couscous

1 tbsp harissa paste, plus extra to serve

55g/2oz butter

3–4 tbsp rosewater (optional)

85g/3oz stoned dates (optional)

salt and pepper

1　Put a large kettle of water on to heat. Heat the oil in a large heavy-based saucepan or casserole over a fairly high heat and brown the chicken portions uniformly on all sides. Do this in batches, if necessary, transferring the browned portions to a bowl placed on one side. While the chicken is browning, trim any excess fat from the lamb and cut it into bite-sized cubes. Then brown these in the same way, adding more oil if necessary.

2　Once all the meat is browned, return to the pan or casserole and pour over the boiling water from the kettle. Place over a high heat to bring to the boil again. Meanwhile, chop the onions and garlic and cut the turnips and carrots into bite-sized chunks. Add all these to the pan with the saffron and other spices and the stock cubes dissolved in a little more hot water. If there is not enough water to cover, add some more.

3　When the contents of the pan or casserole are bubbling, skim off any foam from the surface, then lower the heat to a gentle simmer. Adjust the seasoning if necessary, then cover and leave to simmer for as long as possible, or at least 20 minutes.

4　About 15 minutes before serving the starter, chop the tomatoes and courgettes and add these to the pan with the raisins. Snip in three-quarters of the herbs and add three-quarters of the chickpeas. Mix well. Bring the mixture back to the boil, lower the heat, cover and leave to simmer.

5　Just before serving the starter, pour a kettleful of boiling water over the couscous in a heatproof bowl and leave to steep for 5–15 minutes (according to packet instructions).

6　Drain any excess water from the couscous and fluff it up with a fork. Take 3 or 4 cupfuls of the broth from the stew and mix in some of the harissa to taste (it should be fairly spicy). Stir about one-third of this into the couscous together with the butter, remaining chickpeas, rosewater and dates, if using. Pile it around the edge of a large serving platter. Arrange the meats and vegetables in the middle, moistened with a little of their broth. Snip over the remaining herbs. Serve the remaining harissa-seasoned broth and more harissa paste in separate bowls so your guests can help themselves throughout the meal.

VEGETARIAN SUPPER

Non-vegetarians often find vegetarians tricky to cook for. The problem is how to create a meal that is both interesting and well-balanced. The solution is to opt for quite simple dishes with bold flavours; that way all your guests – whether they eat meat or not – will be satisfied. Certainly, none of your guests will be able to resist the dessert – sweet, gooey brioches filled with a rich concoction of cream and dried fruits soaked in Madeira.

CHICORY WITH
BLUE CHEESE AND
WALNUTS

ROAST OYSTER
MUSHROOMS WITH
TAGLIATELLE

FOR 6-8

SALAD WITH PINK
GRAPEFRUIT DRESSING

BRIOCHE SPLITS

CHICORY WITH BLUE CHEESE AND WALNUTS

Choose a blue cheese with plenty of bite - Roquefort, Gorgonzola or, as here, Stilton. Remember though that some blue cheeses can be quite salty so it is wise to taste the sauce first before adding any extra salt.

55g/2oz butter
115g/4oz walnuts
8 heads of chicory
300ml/¹/₂ pint dry white wine
75g /2¹/₂oz Stilton cheese
salt (optional) and pepper

1 Melt the butter in a large pan.

2 Chop the walnuts coarsely and sauté in the butter for 2 minutes.

3 Cut the chicory in half lengthwise but do not trim the base or the outer leaves will fall off. Put it in the pan, cut side down, and sauté for 1 minute. Pour in the wine and 150ml/¹/₄pt of water. Turn up the heat to bring to the boil, then cover and reduce the heat. Simmer for about 5 minutes or until the chicory has softened but still has a crunch.

4 Using a slotted spoon, lift out the chicory and arrange on a warmed plate.

5 Turn up the heat. Crumble the Stilton and whisk it into the wine, a little at a time, until it has all melted. When all the cheese is incorporated the sauce should be thick.

6 Season to taste and pour over the chicory. Serve immediately.

TO DRINK

A lightly chilled fresh and lively red, such as Chinon, or an Italian Collio Cabernet Franc. A mellow Madeira or a fine dessert sherry with the brioches.

FAST FLOW

1 Preheat oven

2 Prepare and soak dried fruits

3 Boil water for pasta

4 Prepare and roast mushrooms

5 Sauté walnuts

6 Prepare chicory, sauté, then poach

7 Baste brioches with Madeira, whip cream

8 Remove chicory and keep warm

9 Make cheese sauce

10 Check mushrooms; if ready, keep warm

11 Serve chicory

12 Cook pasta

13 Assemble brioches

14 Prepare and dress salad, serve with the pasta

15 Serve brioches

ROAST OYSTER MUSHROOMS WITH TAGLIATELLE

Whether you use fresh or dried pasta is up to you, although it goes without saying that fresh pasta is far quicker to cook. Both must be cooked in plenty of water – about 1.1 litres/2pt for every 115g/4oz of pasta; if you allow as a rough guide between 55–85g/2–3oz of pasta per person, it means that you will need to bring a fair amount of water to the boil. One way to quicken the process is to use both the saucepan and kettle to heat the water.

This recipe works best with flat ribbons of pasta such as tagliatelle, as they provide a bed for the sauce. For a touch of colour, choose a green pasta.

675g/1½lb oyster mushrooms
1 lemon
1 orange
3½ tbsp olive oil
1 tsp sea salt crystals
30g/1oz butter
450–675g/1–1½lb fresh
   tagliatelle
small bunch of fresh chives

1 Preheat the oven 180°C/350°F/ gas 4. Put a pan of water on to boil.

2 Wipe the mushrooms with a clean damp cloth and cut off any thick stems. Squeeze the juice from the lemon and the orange and reserve.

3 Brush the bottom of an ovenproof dish with about 1 tablespoon of the olive oil. Tip the mushrooms into the dish, pour over the remaining olive oil and the orange and lemon juice. Scatter with the salt and, using your hands, toss the mushrooms until they are thoroughly coated. Dot with the butter, then place in the oven. Roast for about 15 minutes or until the mushroom juices start to run.

4 Meanwhile cook the pasta (see introduction above), drain and tip into a serving dish.

5 Remove the mushrooms from the oven and spoon over the pasta. Adjust the seasoning. Snip the chives over the mushrooms. Serve immediately.

SALAD WITH PINK GRAPEFRUIT DRESSING

Just before serving the pasta, empty a couple of bags of ready-washed mixed salad leaves into a large bowl. Snip over a small bunch of flat-leaf parsley and add a chopped ripe avocado. Squeeze the juice from 1 pink grapefruit and mix this in a jar with 7 tablespoons olive oil and some salt and pepper. Pour over the salad and toss lightly to coat.

Roast Oyster Mushrooms with Tagliatelle

Brioche Splits

Do not even think about making your own brioche; it takes far too much time and is unnecessary when you can buy excellent freshly made ones from the supermarket. If you want your pudding to look really dramatic, go for a large brioche, cut into individual servings; although, it has to be said, single small brioches are easier to manage (allow one per person).

100 g/3^1/$_2$oz raisins
100g/3^1/$_2$oz mixed peel
150ml/^{1}/$_4$pt Madeira or sweet sherry
8 mini (or 1 large) brioche(s)
200ml/7fl oz double cream
icing sugar, for dusting

1 Chop the raisins coarsely. Put them in a bowl with the mixed peel and stir in half of the Madeira or sherry. Leave to stand so the fruits soak up the liquid.

2 Cut each brioche in half across the middle and spoon – or paint with a pastry brush, if you prefer – the remaining Madeira over the cut sides.

3 Lightly whip the cream (bear in mind that once the Madeira the dried fruits have been soaking in is added to it, the cream will immediately thicken). Reserve about 1 tablespoon of the fruit mixture. Fold the remainder, together with the Madeira, into the cream.

4 Set aside about 2 generous tablespoons of the cream mixture, then spread the remainder over the cut side of one half of the brioche. Put its lid on top to make a sandwich and flatten it slightly by pressing gently with the palm of your hand.

5 Spoon a dollop of the remaining cream on top of each brioche and scatter over the reserved fruits. Dust each brioche lightly with icing sugar.

THE FATTED CALF

Every so often a situation arises where you have to push the boat out unexpectedly – like, perhaps, a driving test passed on the umpteenth attempt or a wanderer returning home early from their grand trek and looking for their first square meal in months. There is almost always no time to make very special purchases, but if you have a well-stocked store-cupboard and freezer (see pages 8–10) you can come up with a celebration meal that will make anyone feel honoured and welcome.

QUICK CLAM
CHOWDER

INDIVIDUAL BEEF
WELLINGTONS WITH A
MUSTARD SAUCE

FOR 4

STIR-FRIED BRUSSELS
SPROUTS WITH
TOASTED PINE NUTS

TRIFLE DELUXE

QUICK CLAM CHOWDER

Canned baby clams are much more readily available than you might think. These days they can be found in many a corner shop as well as at the delicatessen. They often go under the description *vongole*, their Italian name. Stir them into a basic tomato sauce for a delicious pasta dressing.

3 rashers of smoked streaky bacon
1 large onion
generous pinch of thyme
450g/1lb large old floury
    potatoes
2 heaped tbsp flour
285g/10oz canned baby clams
1 lime
575ml/1pt fish stock
400g/14oz canned chopped plum
    tomatoes
170g/6oz frozen sweetcorn
    kernels
large knob of butter
cayenne pepper or Tabasco sauce
salt and pepper
handful of flat-leaf parsley or
    coriander, to garnish

1   Chop the bacon and put in a large, dry heavy-based saucepan over a moderate heat. Sauté in its own fat until crisp. Remove with a slotted spoon and set aside.

2   Meanwhile, chop the onion. Once the bacon has been removed from the pan, sweat the onion in the bacon fat with the thyme until just soft.

3   While the onion is cooking, peel the potatoes and cube them finely, then add the potato to the onion in the pan

and stir to coat. Sprinkle over the flour and stir well again.

4   Drain the clams, reserving the juice. Put them in a small bowl and squeeze the juice from the lime over them.

5   Pour the clam juice into the soup pan and mix well, then add the fish stock and the tomatoes with their liquid. Bring to the boil. Season to taste and simmer for about 15 minutes.

6   After about 10 minutes of this time, add the sweetcorn, return the bacon to the pan and stir in the butter. Adjust the seasoning, adding a little cayenne or Tabasco for some punch.

7   At the last minute, tip in the clams with the lime juice and stir for a minute over a very gentle heat to warm them through. Snip over some herbs to garnish just before serving.

Variation
Try a little white wine with the stock. For the New England version of this chowder, omit the tomatoes and replace with an equivalent amount of milk or a milk and cream mixture, added at the final stage with the clams; make sure that it does not boil.

FAST FLOW

1
Preheat oven

2
Start making custard

3
Layer trifle

4
Finish custard, pour over trifle and put to chill

5
Cook bacon and onion for chowder and prepare potatoes

6
Add stock, clam juice, tomatoes to chowder and put to simmer

7
Prepare and cook stuffing for Wellingtons and brown steaks

8
Roll out pastry and make parcels

9
Put Wellingtons to bake

10
Add sweetcorn, bacon to chowder

11
Make mustard cream sauce

12
Dry-fry pine nuts. Prepare and grate sprouts

13
Stir in clams, warm through, garnish and serve chowder

14
Stir-fry and finish sprouts, serve with Wellingtons and sauce

15
Whip cream and finish trifle

INDIVIDUAL BEEF WELLINGTONS WITH A MUSTARD SAUCE

Until recently, most cookbooks for the fast cook eschewed all pastries but filo. Since then, however, fresh ready-to-cook puff pastry has appeared beside the boxes of filo in the chill cabinets of our supermarkets. Using it allows glorious little treats like the following, which can be made in very little time. The advantage of individual Wellingtons is that you each get your own *papillote* effect, with all the lovely aroma emerging when the pastry crust is opened – plus everyone gets their share of the delicious juice-soaked pastry base from under the steak.

4–6 shallots

small bunch of flat-leaf parsley

115g/4oz button mushrooms

30g/1oz butter

2–3 tbsp olive oil

4 fillet steaks, each weighing about 170g/6oz

450g/1lb ready-to-roll puff pastry

flour, for dusting

milk, for brushing

salt and pepper

for the Mustard Sauce:

150ml/¼pt crème fraîche

1½ tbsp grainy mustard

1 Preheat the oven to 230°C/450°F/gas 8. Finely chop the shallots, parsley and mushrooms.

2 Melt the butter in a frying pan and sweat the shallots in it briefly, then add the parsley and mushrooms. Stir well and sweat for 2–3 minutes more over a low heat. Season well and turn out on a flat plate to cool.

3 Meanwhile, pour the olive oil into another frying pan or heavy-based saucepan or casserole and place over a high heat. When very hot, brown the steaks well on both sides as quickly as possible. If they are thick, try standing them on edge, using tongs, to brown the sides. Transfer to a flat plate to cool slightly.

4 While the steaks are cooling, roll out the pastry thinly on a lightly floured surface. Cut it into 4 rectangles, each one just big enough to wrap the steaks.

5 When the steaks and stuffing are tepid, set each steak in the centre of a pastry rectangle and pile 2 or 3 spoonfuls of the stuffing on top. Bring up the sides of the pastry to form a parcel and seal by crimping the joining edges like a Cornish pasty, using a little milk to help the edges stick together if necessary. Quickly decorate with a few strokes of a fork and glaze with milk. Cook in the oven for 15 minutes, by which time the pastry should be well risen and golden.

6 While the Wellingtons are baking, make the sauce by stirring any of the remaining stuffing into the pan in which the steaks were browned and deglazing with the crème fraîche. Stir in any juices from the plate on which the steaks stood to cool, together with the mustard. Season to taste and keep warm until the Wellingtons are ready.

Individual Beef Wellingtons

TO DRINK

A well-chilled dry white wine like a Pouilly Fumé with the chowder and a robust red like a good St Émilion with the Wellingtons. If you want to serve anything with the trifle, go for a sparkling celebration wine.

STIR-FRIED BRUSSELS SPROUTS WITH TOASTED PINE NUTS

This recipe is a revelation for all those who hate overcooked sprouts; stir-frying them brings out their inherent nuttiness.

55g/2oz pine nuts
450g/1lb firm Brussels sprouts
large knob of butter
1 tbsp groundnut oil
salt and pepper

1 Put the pine nuts in a dry frying pan and place over a gentle heat. Toast until just golden, tossing them frequently. Set aside.

2 Trim the sprouts and remove the tough outer leaves. Grate the sprouts coarsely into a large bowl.

3 Melt the butter with the oil in a wok or large frying pan over a moderate to high heat. Tip in the grated sprouts and stir-fry for a minute or two, until the shreds are just soft but still crunchy.

4 Season, add the toasted pine nuts and toss well to mix.

TRIFLE DELUXE

A successful trifle is one that is not too sweet, so keep added sugar down, resist the temptation to use a sweet sherry to flavour it, and don't even think of adding jelly!

1 sachet (25g/^{3}/4oz) custard
 powder
575ml/1pt milk
2 tbsp caster sugar
1 packet of trifle sponges
2 punnets of raspberries
2 punnets of blueberries
about 5 tbsp medium or dry (not
 too dry) sherry
300ml/^{1}/2pt double cream
few drops of vanilla essence
candied fruit, for decoration
 (optional)

1 In a heatproof bowl, mix the custard powder smoothly with a spoonful or two of the milk and 1 tablespoon of the sugar. Put the remaining milk on to heat.

2 Line a glass salad bowl, soufflé dish or other suitable serving dish with half the trifle sponges (if they are thick, slice them across into two thinner pieces). Scatter over the raspberries, reserving a few better-looking ones for decoration. Put a layer of half the remaining trifle sponges on top and scatter over the blueberries, reserving a few better-looking ones. Put the remaining trifle sponges on top and sprinkle over the sherry.

3 When the milk is just on the point of boiling, pour it into the custard mixture and stir well. Return to the pan and bring to the boil. Let the mixture boil briefly, stirring continuously, until thick and smooth. Then pour over the trifle. Dig a skewer into the trifle here and there to help the custard permeate the layers. Chill in the refrigerator.

4 Just before serving, whip the cream to soft peaks, adding the vanilla essence and remaining sugar halfway through. Spread over the trifle and decorate with the reserved fruit and some candied fruit, if using.

HOT AND SPICY FEAST

This is an ideal meal for confident cooks to make in front of guests seated at the kitchen table, as it produces such appetizing sizzling noises and wonderful aromas.

Prepare the dessert first and chill it, then make the prawn toasts and serve while they are still piping hot and crisp. The three main-course dishes can then be cooked in rapid succession and kept warm in a low oven while your guests are still finishing their first course. To minimize washing up, make all three dishes in one pan – ideally a wok – wiped well between courses with a wad of paper towels.

QUICK PRAWN TOASTS

PORK MEDALLIONS WITH
GINGER AND ORANGE

STIR-FRIED MIXED LEAVES

CHILLI NOODLES

CHILLED LYCHEE AND
WALNUT CREAM

FOR 6

QUICK PRAWN TOASTS

Buy good fresh firm prawns for this dish: the smaller ones tend to have more flavour. Be sure to rinse them well and pat them quite dry with paper towels to get rid of any lingering moisture. If you use frozen prawns, make sure they are well defrosted and drained – you will also need about twice the weight specified here, as once their ice glaze melts away you will be surprised at how little is left.

4 spring onions

225g/8oz peeled cooked prawns

small sprig of coriander

2 tsp cornflour

$1/2$ tsp sugar

2 tsp light soy sauce

1 tsp dry sherry

good dash of Tabasco sauce (optional)

$1/2$ tsp Oriental sesame oil

1 egg

12 thin-cut slices of day-old white bread

4 tbsp sesame seeds

salt and pepper

groundnut oil, for frying

lime wedges, to serve (optional)

extra coriander leaves, to garnish (optional)

1 Coarsely snip the spring onions into the bowl of a food processor and add the prawns, coriander, cornflour, sugar, soy sauce, sherry, Tabasco (if using) to taste and the sesame oil and whizz until the spring onions and prawns are finely chopped.

2 Add the egg, season well with salt and pepper to taste and whizz again briefly to a fairly smooth paste.

3 Pour the groundnut oil into a wok or large frying pan to a depth of about 1cm/$1/2$in and heat until a small cube of bread added to the pan browns in about 40 seconds.

4 While the oil is heating, cut the crusts off the bread and spread each slice with some of the prawn mixture. Sprinkle the tops with sesame seeds.

5 Cut each slice of bread into 4 triangles or strips. Fry them in batches, paste side down, for about 1 minute and then turn them over and fry the other side very briefly (about 15–20 seconds), until golden brown. As soon as each batch is cooked, remove from the pan, drain on paper towels and keep, uncovered, in a warm place.

6 Serve the toasts as soon as they are all cooked, with lime wedges and coriander leaves, if using.

Variations
Use parsley instead of coriander; vary the flavour of the prawn mixture by adding some fresh root ginger or even some chopped cooked bacon; use a pastry cutter to cut the toasts into crescent shapes.

FAST FLOW

1 Make lychee and walnut cream and chill

2 Prepare pork medallions and marinate

3 Put noodles to soak

4 Prepare leaves

5 (Remember to drain noodles before they get too soft)

6 Prepare chillies (and wash hands)

7 Make and serve prawn toasts

8 Cook pork medallions and keep warm

9 Stir-fry noodles and keep warm

10 Cook leaves and serve with pork and noodles

PORK MEDALLIONS WITH GINGER AND ORANGE

This weight of pork tenderloin is equivalent to about $1^1/_2$ average-size whole fillets. If you buy frozen fillets they are very easy to slice into neat chunks while still frozen and they then defrost very rapidly.

675g/1$^1/_2$lb pork tenderloin

1 lime

4cm/1$^1/_2$in piece of fresh ginger

3 garlic cloves

5 tbsp orange juice

1 tbsp rice vinegar or red wine vinegar

2 tbsp clear honey

1 tbsp dark soy sauce

1 tbsp cornflour

3 tbsp dry sherry

about 3 tbsp groundnut oil

salt and pepper

1   Trim the tenderloin and cut it into 2–2.5cm/$^3/_4$–1in slices.

2   Arrange these on a piece of baking paper or metal foil, place another piece of paper or foil over them and flatten with a meat mallet or the flat of a large heavy kitchen knife.

3   Layer the pork medallions in a shallow bowl.

4   Pare the outer zest from the lime with a small sharp knife or vegetable peeler. Peel the ginger and chop it coarsely. Put the lime zest and ginger in a food processor with the garlic and whizz until finely chopped.

5   Add the juice from the lime, half the orange juice, the vinegar, honey, soy sauce, cornflour, half the sherry, and salt and pepper to taste. Whizz briefly until well mixed.

6   Pour the mixture over the pork medallions, toss well to coat and leave

to marinate for at least 15 minutes, turning the pieces of pork from time to time to make sure they are well covered.

7   Heat some of the oil in a wok or large frying pan over a moderate to high heat and fry the pork medallions in batches for about $1^1/_2$ minutes on each side until nicely browned. (Don't bother to drain the medallions too thoroughly as you take them from the marinade, just lift them out of the bowl and leave any marinade solids clinging to them.) Transfer to a dish in a warm place as soon as they are cooked.

8   When all the pork is fried, pour the remaining marinade (solids included) into the pan together with the remaining orange juice and sherry and deglaze the pan with it.

9   Boil rapidly until the liquid has a good sauce-like consistency and then return the pork to the pan and toss to coat well and heat through. Transfer to a warm serving dish.

Quick Prawn Toasts (see page 57)

TO DRINK

One is traditionally advised against drinking wine with hot and spicy food and told to stick to beer or tea, but a good dry rosé – particularly a rosé champagne – works well throughout this meal. A good-quality dry cider would also be a nice alternative – try one of the excellent new English *méthode champenoise* ciders.

STIR-FRIED MIXED LEAVES

You can save a lot of time by using sachets of ready-washed leaves for this recipe, as most supermarkets produce more or less the sort of mix required. What you need are some deep green leaves, like spinach, chard or watercress, mixed in with some crisp-textured paler leaves like Chinese cabbage or chicory (some crisper lettuce leaves, such as cos, will do). Coarser leaves like spring greens and dandelion leaves will work, but they need to be finely shredded. Add some red chicory or radicchio for colour. Whatever you choose, aim for a balance of tastes, textures and colours.

**675g/1$^{1}/_{2}$lb mixed leaves
   (see above)
2–3 tbsp vegetable oil
3 spring onions
$^{1}/_{2}$ tsp sugar
1$^{1}/_{2}$ tbsp light soy sauce
1 tsp Oriental sesame oil
salt and pepper**

1 If necessary, wash the leaves and pat dry. Remove any coarser ribs and stalks with a sharp knife.

2 Heat some of the vegetable oil in a wok or large frying pan and toss in half the leaves (if not using a bag of mixed leaves, make these the crisper leaves). Stir-fry rapidly over a high heat until just wilting (this should take between 40 seconds and 1 minute).

3 Using a slotted spoon, transfer the cooked leaves to a warmed serving bowl or dish and keep warm.

4 Cook the remaining leaves in the same way (but even more briefly if you are using your own mix), adding more vegetable oil if necessary. Remove the leaves and transfer to the serving dish.

5 Snip the spring onions into the oil and stir-fry them briefly, then add the sugar, salt and pepper to taste and the light soy sauce and stir-fry briefly until well mixed.

6 Pour this over the leaves in the serving bowl, drizzle over the sesame oil and toss well to coat.

Variation
An easy way to add a splash of colour is to replace the spring onions with a sliced red onion.

HINT

If you are catering for health-conscious guests who are wary of an all-fried meal, replace the oil with a good vegetable stock. Finish the meal with a fresh fruit salad.

CHILLI NOODLES

The advantage of Chinese noodles is that they just need soaking in boiling water rather than actual cooking.

225g/8oz Chinese rice or egg
noodles
2–3 small red chilli peppers
2 tbsp groundnut oil
1 tbsp light soy sauce
1 tbsp chilli oil or Chinese
chilli paste

1 Soak the noodles in boiling water for a minute or so less than the time suggested by the packet instructions (usually about 4–8 minutes) and drain well; they should still have a bit of bite.

2 While the noodles are soaking, deseed and very finely shred the chilli peppers (be sure to wash your hands thoroughly immediately afterwards and do not touch your eyes or other sensitive areas until you have).

3 Heat the groundnut oil in a wok or large frying pan and fry the chilli shreds very briefly.

4 Stir in the soy sauce and chilli oil or paste followed by the drained noodles and stir-fry well until all the noodles are well coated and heated through.

Variation
Leave a few chilli shreds uncooked and scatter over the noodles before serving.

CHILLED LYCHEE AND WALNUT CREAM

This creamy dessert is the ideal complement to a wonderfully pungent, hot main course.

575ml/1pt chilled whipping cream
1 tbsp orange-flower water or
orange-flavoured liqueur
450g/1lb canned lychees in syrup
about 115g/4oz walnut halves
grated citrus zest, for decoration
(optional)

1 Whip the cream until it stands in stiff peaks.

2 Add the orange-flower water or liqueur and sweeten the cream with a little of the syrup from the lychees.

3 Spoon into small ramekins, coupes, bowls or dessert dishes.

4 Drain the lychees completely and coarsely chop the walnuts.

5 Distribute the lychees evenly over the cream. Scatter over the walnuts and chill until ready to serve.

6 Grate over a little lemon, lime or orange zest before serving, if desired.

If Time Allows
Instead of chopping the walnuts, insert a walnut half into each of the lychees (you may have to widen the slits with your fingers first).

Finger and fork food

20 IDEAS FOR NO-COOK AND STORE-CUPBOARD CANAPÉS

Believe it or not, canapés can be very fast to make, particularly if you work on the principle of a factory assembly line. First get your bases organized and spread them out evenly on your work space, then make the toppings and finally put the two together by spooning the topping carefully on to the bases and pressing it down gently. And as you are working in miniature, make sure you use a teaspoon. Decorate with a leaf or the tiniest sprig of an appropiate fresh herb (one that has been used in the recipe or that will complement the topping).

Arrange the canapés in rows on a large serving plate. Never put too many on at once - not only does this make them much more difficult to get hold of, but they can start to look too much of a jumble. As for how many different types of canapés to serve, that is up to you and the time you have available; as a rough guide, no less than two and no more than six types should be about right. Quantities depend on how long you plan to entertain your friends and what else you plan to serve, but the general rule of appetite is 6–8 canapés per person. And remember, never make your canapés too big; one or at the very most two bites is as large as they should be.

BASES

Most canapés need a base of some sort or another as a means of holding the topping. They can either be fairly rigid or with a hollow and, for our purposes, they fall into two categories - fresh or baked. Many toppings can be used on either type of base, so you can use whatever you have to hand.

For fresh bases, use peeled cucumber slices cut to about 1–1.5cm/^{1}/2–^{3}/4in thick and with a little of the seed hollowed out for the topping, or celery sticks filled down the centre. Cherry tomatoes or small potatoes can be hollowed out, but this is a fiddly and time-consuming operation; it is far quicker and easier to use the leaves broken off a head of chicory, radicchio, Little Gem, iceberg or cos lettuce as they all make suitable cups.

For baked bases, buy mini oatcakes, pastry cups or shells, mini vol-au-vents, or baby scones and cut them in half. A bought focaccia can be cut into small squares or any shape you fancy; baguettes or ciabatta can be cut into small slices, then lightly brushed with olive oil and baked in the oven. Alternatively, you can make your own bread discs from thinly sliced bread. Cut out discs with a 2.5cm/1in pastry cutter (you should be able to get about 7–8 discs per slice), mix a crushed clove of garlic into a cup of olive oil, paint the bread discs on both sides with this and bake them on a baking sheet in a preheated oven (190°C/375°F/gas 5) for about 15 minutes until crisp and golden. They can be prepared a couple of days in advance provided you store them in an airtight tin.

TOPPINGS

(each makes enough for 24 canapés, unless otherwise stated)

Blue Cheese and Bacon

Place 55g/2oz blue cheese in a bowl and mash it with a fork, stirring in 1 tbsp of single cream. Grill 2–3 rashers of streaky bacon until crisp, then chop the rashers into small pieces. Spoon the cheese mixture on to the base and sprinkle the bacon pieces over the top.

Baked Garlic

Preheat the oven to 190°C/375°F/gas 5. Break a large head of garlic into cloves. Using a pastry brush, paint the cloves with olive oil, place on a baking sheet and bake for 15–20 minutes. Extract the garlic pulp by slitting the skin and pressing it out into a bowl. Spread the garlic pulp on to a bread disc and decorate with slithers of sun-dried tomato, olive, or a basil leaf.

Goats' Cheese Crostini

Preheat the oven to 190°C/375°F/gas 5 or heat the grill to high. Take a log of matured goats' cheese about 3–4cm/1–1^1/2in diameter, weighing about 225g/8oz. Cut the log into thin slices - at least 12 - and lay each on a slice of French bread. Place under the grill or in the preheated oven for 7–10 minutes, until the cheese starts to bubble. Decorate with sprigs of thyme.

Baby Artichokes and Cream Cheese

Take 55g/2oz fresh cream cheese and spread it thinly on bread bases of your choice. Take a jar of baby artichokes in oil, drain about 4 and cut them into slithers. Lay an artichoke slither on top of each cream cheese canapé. Finely chop a small bunch of parsley, sprinkle it over the top, then finish off with some freshly ground black pepper.

Ricotta and Pesto

Take 85g/3oz ricotta cheese and mash it with 2 tablespoons of bought pesto, some salt and freshly ground pepper. Spoon over a base of your choice and decorate with torn basil leaves.

Smoked Venison and Fresh Parsley

Take 115g/4oz smoked venison, chop it finely and place in a bowl. Stir in 1 tablespoon of olive oil, 1 teaspoon of lemon juice, 1 chopped spring onion and a small bunch of finely chopped flat-leaf parsley. Season with black pepper, spoon on to the prepared base and decorate with a single parsley leaf.

Scrambled Eggs with Smoked Salmon and Dill

Make scrambled eggs with 2 eggs and about 15g/^{1}/2oz butter. Just as the egg is setting, remove from the heat, stir in 1 tablespoon single cream and spoon on to a bread base of your choice. Cut 55g/2oz smoked salmon into strips and lay on top of the eggs. Decorate with a sprig of dill.

Avocado and Smoked Chicken

Peel and chop 1 small ripe avocado, then cut 55g/2oz of smoked chicken into strips and mix together. Make a vinaigrette with 2 tablespoons of olive oil, 2 teaspoons of lemon juice and the grated rind of ^{1}/2 a lemon. Pour the vinaigrette over the avocado and chicken and combine all ingredients. Spoon on to a base of your choice.

Smoked Eel with Crème Fraîche and Horseradish

Take 85g/3oz smoked eel fillets and cut into thin strips. Arrange the eel strips on a bread base. In a small bowl, mix 4 tablespoons of crème fraîche with 1 tablespoon of grated horseradish and a small bunch of chopped dill. Drizzle this mixture over the eel, season with black pepper and top with a sprig of dill.

Parma Ham, Ricotta and Olive Spread

Beat 3 tablespoons of green olive paste with 55g/2oz ricotta and 1 tablespoon of olive oil. Shred 55g/2oz Parma ham and beat it into the mixture. Season with black pepper and spoon on to a base of your choice (use only a tiny amount as this spread is strongly flavoured). Top with a majoram leaf.

Artichoke, Egg and Fresh Chive Paste

Hard-boil 2 eggs, then peel and mash them while still warm. Tip the egg into a small bowl, then stir in 1 tablespoon bought artichoke paste, a dash of lemon juice, 1 tablespoon olive oil and a small bunch of chopped chives. Spoon on to a base of your choice and decorate with snipped chives.

Caper and Anchovy Spread

Chop 1 bunch of flat-leaf parsley, 1 spring onion, 1 teaspoon of drained capers, 1 teaspoon of pine nuts and 2 anchovies and mix together in a bowl. Alternatively, whizz them in the food processor (but take care not to over-process). Stir in 1 tablespoon of olive oil and 1 teaspoon of balsamic vinegar, then spoon on to a base of your choice.

FAST FINGER FOOD

You do not always need to stick to the formula of base and topping when making canapés for drinks parties. These simple, speedy ideas make an unusual change and can be prepared in next to no time. Each one serves 12 people unless otherwise stated.

Baby New Potatoes with Sour Cream Dip

Choose tiny potatoes and give them a rinse under cold running water. You do not need to peel them – their skins are full of flavour and make them look far more attractive if left on.

900g/2lb small potatoes
2 spring onions
small bunch of dill
2–3 sun-dried tomatoes in oil, drained
1 medium tub of sour cream
salt and pepper

1 Boil the potatoes in lightly salted water, drain and leave to cool slightly.
2 Meanwhile, finely chop the spring onions, the dill and the drained sun-dried tomatoes and stir into the sour cream.
3 Season to taste and tip out into a bowl placed in the middle of a large plate. Arrange the potatoes around.

Marinated olives

Plain olives in brine are a good deal cheaper than the ready-dressed olives you see at delicatessen counters. You can make up batches of these olives as you want them or mix larger quantities – they will keep for up to a week in the refrigerator.

for the green olives:

115g/4oz green olives in brine, drained

1 small lemon

1 garlic clove

small bunch of marjoram

1 tbsp extra virgin olive oil

for the black olives:

115g/4oz black olives, drained

1 orange

1 tsp pink peppercorns

small bunch flat-leaf parsley

1 tbsp extra virgin olive oil

1   Put the green olives in a bowl. Roughly chop the lemon, crush the garlic and chop the marjoram, then add all these ingredients to the olives together with the olive oil. Mix together thoroughly.

2   Put the black olives in another bowl. Zest the orange, coarsely crush the peppercorns and finely chop the parsley. Add all these ingredients to the olives, pour over the olive oil and stir thoroughly to mix.

Roasted Almonds

Buy unsalted peeled almonds – flaked or halves are fine but remember they will only need a few minutes in the oven. Any leftovers can be stored in an airtight container.

450g/1lb peeled almonds

1 tsp sea salt

1 tsp ground cumin

oil, for greasing

1   Preheat the oven to 200°C/400°F/gas 6. Scatter the nuts on a lightly greased baking tray. Mix the salt and cumin, pour over the nuts and turn them with your hands so they are well coated.

2   Bake for 5–7 minutes, or until they just start to turn colour.

Salami Plate

The easiest canapé of them all. For a really appealing plate, buy several different sliced salamis – including some Italian prosciutto – allowing about 15g/$\frac{1}{2}$oz per person and arrange them neatly on a plate.

Parma Ham Pears

Take 4 firm pears and 115g/4oz parma ham, then cut the pears in half and remove the cores. Slice the pears into slithers about 2.5cm/1in thick. Wrap each slither with a thinly cut slice of Parma ham (depending on the size of the pear slithers, you may need to cut the slices of ham in half); start at one end, leaving the tip of the pear free, then twist the ham around the pear until you almost get to the other end. Dust with finely ground black pepper.

Michelle's Hot Artichoke Dip

Serve this creamy dip straight from the oven with crisp crackers or taco chips.

2 x 400g/14oz cans artichoke hearts

300ml/$\frac{1}{2}$pt mayonnaise

100g/3$\frac{1}{2}$oz Parmesan cheese

salt and black pepper

1   Preheat the oven to 180°C/350°F/gas 4.

2   Grate the Parmesan, then put all the ingredients in a food processor and whizz until everything is well mixed.

3   Transfer to a baking dish and bake for 30 minutes. Turn out into a bowl and serve immediately.

Baked Camembert

Choose a ripe but reasonably firm Camembert about 15cm/6in in diameter. Sometimes finding a ripe one can be a bit of a problem, so it might be a good idea to buy one a few days in advance and leave it to ripen. Using a sharp knife, slice the top off the Camembert, then lay it back on top of the cheese. Bake in a preheated oven at 200°C/400°F/gas 6 for about 15 minutes. To serve, remove the lid, arrange the cheese on a plate surrounded with small water biscuits or crackers and let everyone dip into the cheese – which will be gloriously melted and runny.

Kipper Dip

Surround a bowl of this quick smoked fish dip with sticks of raw vegetables and small crackers for dipping.

85g/3oz kipper fillets

1 lemon

small bunch of watercress

dash of dry Martini or dry white wine

85g/3oz curd cheese

1 tbsp double cream

black pepper

1   Put the kipper fillets in the food processor with the juice of the lemon, the watercress leaves and all the other ingredients. Whizz well until you reach a creamy consistency.

2   Check the seasoning and turn out into a bowl to serve.

THE AMAZING BUFFET SPREAD THAT APPEARED FROM NOWHERE

Nothing will enhance your reputation as a cook more than deftly dealing in a fairly formal manner with an unexpected occasion - say, throwing a surprise party for someone or holding an important meeting at your place over supper.

This impressive spread can be put together with predominantly store-cupboard and refrigerator staples, yet gives the appearance of having been planned at committee level. Omit the fish from the Salade Niçoise and add a spoonful of capers, and substitute aubergines for the chicken in the Tetrazzini and you have a buffet that vegetarians can enjoy.

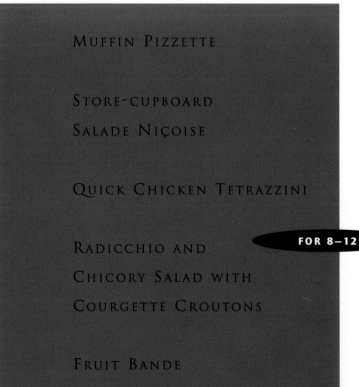

MUFFIN PIZZETTE

STORE-CUPBOARD
SALADE NIÇOISE

QUICK CHICKEN TETRAZZINI

RADICCHIO AND
CHICORY SALAD WITH
COURGETTE CROUTONS

FOR 8–12

FRUIT BANDE

MUFFIN PIZZETTE

You can have all sorts of alternative toppings on these little pizzas: add some thinly sliced salami or pepperoni, or some sliced mushrooms or red onions (or both) lightly sautéed in a little butter and oil. You can even make them *alla marinara* with some tiny prawns and a few dill sprigs.

6 muffins
2 tbsp tomato paste
150ml/¼pt passata
generous pinch of sugar
1 tsp dried oregano
½ tsp balsamic vinegar
good pinch of cayenne pepper
1 Mozzarella cheese
12 stoned black olives
salt and pepper

1 Preheat the grill to medium.

2 Split the muffins and toast them, flat sides up, until lightly browned.

3 Meanwhile, in a small pan over a moderate heat, mix the tomato paste into the passata, together with the sugar, oregano and vinegar. Season to taste with salt, pepper and cayenne.

4 Spread the tomato sauce over the untoasted sides of the muffins, then slice the cheese into strips and arrange on top. Dot with the olives.

5 Return to the grill and toast until the cheese is bubbling.

TO DRINK

A good medium-bodied dry white wine like an Italian Orvieto, or a Provençal rosé

FAST FLOW

1 Preheat oven for bande; heat pans of water for potatoes and eggs

2 Prepare pastry and put in oven

3 Cook potatoes and eggs. Prepare vegetables for Salade Niçoise

4 Put water to heat for pasta and heat chicken stock for Tetrazzini

5 Prepare and cook mushrooms, prepare chicken

6 Glaze pastry; return to oven

7 Remove pastry from oven; let cool

8 Stir-fry chicken; make chicken sauce

9 Preheat grill; prepare leaves for radicchio salad; prepare courgettes; assemble Salade Niçoise

10 Toast muffins. Make pizzette sauce

11 Fry courgette strips

12 Arrange pizzette toppings and grill; put pasta to cook

13 Drain pasta; assemble Tetrazzini and finish under grill

14 Dress and finish salads. Top bande with cream and fruit

STORE-CUPBOARD SALADE NIÇOISE

I t is amazing how delicious and refreshing a salad made with a large percentage of canned vegetables can be. The secret is knowing when to use tinned products and when to use fresh. This is one occasion when fresh tomatoes are a must, no matter now tasty canned Italian plum tomatoes are. Don't be tempted by tinned potatoes: the warmth and texture of the freshly cooked spud are essential to this salad. And don't even consider canned green beans, though cannellini beans from a tin will do if you can't find flageolets.

450g/1lb potatoes, preferably small
6 eggs
400g/14oz canned sweet red peppers
400g/14oz canned artichoke hearts
400g/14oz canned flageolets
1 large cos lettuce, or 4 Little Gems
bunch of spring onions
1 cucumber
450g/1lb tomatoes
400g/14oz canned tuna chunks in oil
100g/3^1/2 oz canned or bottled anchovies
225g/8oz stoned black olives, preferably garlic-flavoured
several large handfuls of fresh herbs, e.g. flat-leaf parsley, chives, basil, chervil and tarragon

for the dressing:
2 garlic cloves
150ml/^{1}/4pt extra-virgin olive oil
2 tbsp white wine vinegar
2 tbsp lemon juice
salt and pepper

1 Put a pan of salted water on to heat. Peel the potatoes, if necessary, and add them when the water is boiling. Put another pan of water on to heat and add the eggs. Only allow the potatoes to cook until barely tender – they must not become mushy. The eggs should be boiled for 12 minutes only.

2 Drain all the canned vegetables. Cut the peppers into strips and the artichoke hearts in half. Put all the vegetables in a colander and rinse under a cold tap. Leave to drain.

3 Remove any wilted or damaged leaves from the lettuce(s), separate the leaves and rinse well. Spin or pat dry with paper towels. Shred the leaves into the bottom of 1 or 2 large salad bowls or dishes. Trim the spring onions and snip them over the leaves. Slice the cucumber lengthwise into 2 or 3 long slices and then cut these into long strips. Finally, cut across into 2cm/^{3}/4in chunks. Add to the bowl(s). Quarter the tomatoes and halve these quarters again if large. Add to the bowl(s).

4 Drain the tuna. Flake one can into the salad bowl(s). Snip the anchovies

into pieces and add half of them to the bowl(s) along with the olives. Snip in half the herbs.

5 Spin or pat dry the drained tinned vegetables and add these to the salad.

6 By this time the potatoes and eggs should be cooked. Drain the potatoes and dry briefly over a low heat, then leave to cool on a flat plate. Drain and submerge the eggs in cold water to prevent them from cooking further.

7 To make the dressing, crush the garlic into the oil, add the vinegar and lemon juice and season to taste. Mix well to a smooth emulsion and adjust the seasoning.

8 Cut the potatoes into bite-sized chunks if necessary and add these to the salad. Pour the dressing over the salad and toss well to mix. Taste and adjust the seasoning again if necessary.

9 Shell the eggs, cut into quarters and arrange these over the top of the salad together with the remaining tuna, olives and anchovies. Snip over the remaining herbs.

QUICK
CHICKEN TETRAZZINI

Chicken Tetrazzini was a favourite party dish in the 1960s, but it did take a long time to make. This version has most of the richness and flavour of the original, but can be put together in a fraction of the time. If money is no object, some thinly sliced white truffles (or even a small tin of them) stirred into the chicken at the last minute will make this a really memorable dish.

575ml/1pt chicken or vegetable stock

85g/3oz butter

2 lemons

350g/12oz mushrooms, preferably organic brown-cap

6–8 chicken (preferably corn-fed) breasts

dash of olive oil

3 tbsp flour

300ml/1/2pt crème fraîche

150ml/1/4pt Marsala or medium-dry sherry

1/2 nutmeg

450g/1lb fresh spaghetti or tagliarini

55g/2oz Parmesan cheese

salt and pepper

1 Put a pan of salted water on to heat for the pasta (if preferred, heat some of the water in a kettle to speed things up). Put the chicken stock on to heat in a saucepan.

2 Melt half the butter in a large frying pan over a gentle heat and squeeze in the juice from the lemons.

3 Wipe the mushrooms and thinly slice them. Add to the butter and lemon juice and sauté until soft.

4 While the mushrooms are cooking, remove and discard any skin from the chicken. Cut the breasts into thin strips.

5 Remove the mushrooms with their juices from the frying pan and keep warm. Melt the remaining butter in the pan with a dash of oil and stir-fry the chicken strips briefly until uniformly white and just stiff (do not over-cook the strips, as they will be cooked through later with the sauce).

6 Sprinkle the flour over the chicken and stir-fry briefly to cook the flour.

Gradually add the hot stock, stirring constantly, until the sauce becomes smooth. Simmer gently until the sauce thickens.

7 Stir in the crème fraîche and the Marsala or sherry. Grate in some nutmeg to taste and adjust the seasoning. Leave to simmer very gently. Preheat the grill to high.

8 While the sauce is simmering, cook the pasta in rapidly boiling water until just *al dente*; it should take no more than a minute or two. Drain well, return to the pan and pour half the sauce into it. Add the reserved mushrooms with their liquid and toss the pasta well. Turn into a large, deep, warmed heatproof serving dish.

9 Make a well in the centre of the pasta and pour in the chicken and remaining sauce.

10 Grate the Parmesan over the top of the pasta and chicken and flash briefly under the grill to brown the cheese lightly.

RADICCHIO AND CHICORY SALAD WITH COURGETTE CROUTONS

2–3 heads of radicchio
2–3 heads of chicory
bunch of watercress or baby spinach
6 medium courgettes
55g/2oz flour
1 tbsp paprika
2–3 tbsp sunflower oil
4 tbsp extra virgin olive oil
3 tbsp walnut oil
salt and pepper
1 large lemon

1 Separate the leaves of the radicchio and chicory. Rinse and pat dry or just wipe with damp paper towels. Rinse and dry the watercress or spinach. Arrange the leaves in a medley on a large shallow serving dish.

2 Trim the courgettes and cut into thin julienne strips (like thin French fries) about 2.5cm/1in long.

3 Season the flour and mix in the paprika. Put it in a large plastic bag and add the courgette strips. Close the bag and shake to coat the strips evenly.

4 In a large frying pan, heat the sunflower oil over a moderate to high heat. Fry the floured courgette strips (in 2 batches if necessary) until browned and crisp.

5 While the courgette strips are cooking, mix the extra-virgin olive oil and walnut oil and drizzle this over the salad, then season generously.

6 When the courgette croutons are all cooked, scatter them over the salad. Squeeze lemon juice over the top and serve immediately.

FRUIT BANDE

Made with ready-to-roll puff pastry, now available in supermarket chill cabinets, this simple, classic fruit tart always impresses.

450g/1lb ready-to-roll puff pastry
30g/1oz unsalted butter
450ml/1¹/₂pt crème fraîche
3 tbsp caster sugar
few drops of good-quality vanilla essence
1 tbsp brandy
450g/1lb strawberries
450g/1lb ripe nectarines
5–6 heaped tbsp apricot jam
1–2 tbsp orange liqueur

1 Preheat the oven to 220°C/425°F/ gas 7. Roll out the pastry to a rectangle about 45 x 30cm (18 x 12in). Crimp the edges to make a rim and prick the rest of the pastry well with a fork. Place on a baking tray and bake for 5 minutes.

2 Melt the butter in a small pan. Remove the pastry from the oven, prick all over again and brush liberally with the melted butter. Return to the oven for another 7–9 minutes, until well browned. Transfer to a wire rack to cool.

3 Whip the cream lightly, adding the sugar, vanilla and brandy. Hull the strawberries, wash and pat dry if necessary. Stone and slice the nectarines.

4 When the pastry is cool to the touch, spread the flavoured cream all over the inner base. Arrange the fruit in diagonal bands across it.

5 Melt the apricot jam in a small pan, stir in the orange liqueur and use to glaze the fruit.

LAZY GOURMET BARBECUE

On a good day – one with fine weather and people in the right mood – barbecuing can be the essence of relaxed cooking. This does not necessarily mean playing it safe with beefburgers. But since all the climate and equipment variables leave you not quite as in control as you would be in your own kitchen, forget subtlety and opt for a menu which delivers strong flavours and is quickly and simply prepared. For the dessert, barbecuing bananas in their skins really brings out their aroma and sweetness; a simple rum-flavoured crème fraîche intensifies the taste.

TO DRINK

Don't forget the ice cubes! Together with plenty of chilled water, serve a choice of ice-cold designer bottles of lager (this is a good time to experiment) and/or rosé wine, perhaps from Provence or Southwest France.

PEPPER WEDGES WITH CHILLIED AVOCADO SALSA

BARBECUED ITALIAN SAUSAGES

WARM SALAD OF WILTED SPINACH

FOR 6

GRILLED SPLIT BANANAS WITH RUM-FLAVOURED CRÈME FRAÎCHE

PEPPER WEDGES WITH CHILLIED AVOCADO SALSA

Warm sweet peppers and spicy chilled mashed avocados complement each other in a gutsy combination that will get the tastebuds going.

6–8 sweet peppers (e.g. 3 red, 1 green and 2 yellow)
1 tbsp olive oil
1 spring onion, white and green parts, snipped (optional)
salt and pepper

for the avocado salsa:
1 lime
2 large (or 3 small) ripe Hass avocados
1 garlic clove, crushed
2 tbsp olive oil, plus 1 extra tbsp to serve
pinch of hot chilli powder, or ¼ tsp chilli paste
¼ tsp ground cumin
salt and pepper

1 Preheat the grill until very hot (or alternatively use the barbecue) and char the peppers until the skin blisters. This will take several minutes – allow for about 5 minutes each side and carefully turn over halfway through. Remove from the heat, cover with a thick layer of newspaper and leave until cool enough to handle.

2 Make the avocado salsa either in advance or while the peppers are charring and resting. Grate a little lime zest and squeeze to extract the juice. Peel and stone the avocados. Whizz in the food processor or mash with a fork until coarsely puréed – stop while a few chunks of avocado still remain.

3 Smash and peel the garlic, then coarsely chop it. In a bowl, combine the garlic, olive oil and chilli. Add the rough avocado purée and mix with a fork. Now stir in the lime juice and zest and the ground cumin.

4 Season to taste with salt and pepper. Stir in a little extra olive oil. Cover with clingfilm and put in the freezer for a few minutes until ready to use. If preparing ahead, chill in the coldest part of the refrigerator. Stir the mixture and adjust the seasoning before serving.

5 Peel the peppers (it does not matter if some of the skin remains). Slit them open, cut out the core and scoop out the seeds. Divide each pepper lengthwise into 4 wedges. Arrange skinned side up on a serving dish. Drizzle with the olive oil and season again. Scatter over the spring onion, if using, and serve with the salsa.

FAST FLOW

1 Preheat barbecue

2 Make and chill avocado salsa

3 Flavour and chill crème fraîche

4 Chill drinks

5 Assemble all necessary equipment and ingredients

6 Preheat grill (if using)

7 Char and cover sweet peppers

8 Start cooking sausages

9 Wilt and dress spinach

10 Peel, core, deseed and cut sweet peppers

11 Barbecue bananas after eating the main courses

BARBECUED ITALIAN SAUSAGES

U se highly seasoned, top-quality, small fat Italian cooking sausages, the longer *luganega*, or spicy designer sausages.

about 675g/1¹/₂lb good Italian cooking sausages (see above)

Barbecue the sausages as slowly as possible, turning frequently so that they are evenly cooked and not too charred. If using a grill, preheat until hot, then reduce the heat and grill for 20–30 minutes until cooked. Turn frequently and reduce the heat a little halfway through cooking to prevent burning.

WARM SPINACH SALAD

3 tbsp olive oil
2-3 garlic cloves
3 tbsp pine nuts
about 600g/1¹/₄lb ready-to-use baby spinach leaves
1-2 tbsp balsamic vinegar
1 tbsp soy sauce
salt and pepper
warm focaccia, to serve

1   In a large sauté or frying pan, heat half the oil. Smash and peel the garlic, chop finely and add to the oil. Add the pine nuts and sauté for 1 minute over a moderate heat. (All this can be done over the barbecue grill.)

2   Tip in the spinach, spread it out and leave for 1 minute. Stir for another 2 minutes until the spinach wilts a little.

3   Drizzle in half the balsamic vinegar, stir and season lightly. Transfer to a warmed serving dish. Add the rest of the oil to the pan. Tilt the pan around over the heat, then sprinkle in the rest of the vinegar, the soy sauce and 2 tablespoons of water. Stir to mix and heat through, then drizzle the juices over the spinach. Serve as soon as possible with wedges of warm focaccia.

GRILLED SPLIT BANANAS WITH RUM-FLAVOURED CRÈME FRAÎCHE

medium tub of crème fraîche
2 tbsp rum
6 ripe but firm bananas

1   Whisk the crème fraîche until light and smooth. Stir in the rum, whisk again lightly and chill until needed.

2   Put the unpeeled bananas on the barbecue grill away from any flames. After about 5 minutes, turn over.

Continue barbecuing for a few minutes until the skin blisters and splits. Using a sharp knife or scissors, split open the bananas to make a boat.

3   Spoon the chilled crème fraîche over the bananas and serve.

Pepper Wedges with Chillied Avocado Salsa (see page 75)

Dinner parties

FLEXIBLE FAST DINNER PARTY

- Clear Broth with Thai Spices
- Mussels with Lemon Grass and Noodles
- Crisp Vegetable Medley
- Instant Fruit Tart of the Season

SUMMER AFTER-THEATRE SUPPER

- Chilled Avocado, Tomato and Coriander Soup
- Grilled Duck Breasts with a Warm Courgette and Pear Salad
- Orange and Pistachio Granita

MORE DASH THAN CASH

- Leeks with Caper and Egg Sauce
- Chicken Livers with Bacon and Tomatoes on Pasta
- Green Salad with Herbed Olive Oil
- Hot Apples in Cider

WINTER MEDITERRANEAN VEGETARIAN FEAST

- Courgette Soup with Sage Croutons
- Watercress, Orange and Radish Salade Marocaine
- Aubergine Tian
- Provençal Dessert Plate

ELEGANT BUT SUBSTANTIAL

- Crab Filo Tarts
- Pan-grilled Lamb Steaks with Apricot Confit
- Pilaff Mould with Watercress Salad
- Vanilla Ice Cream dressed with Passion Fruit

SUMMER EVENING AL FRESCO

- Warm Salmon Salad
- Chervil New Potatoes
- Chicken Breasts with Cucumber and Tarragon Sauce
- Summer Berry Brûlée

FLEXIBLE FAST DINNER PARTY

With a built-in starter, ingredients that are easy to stretch or to vary and a dessert that can be adapted to suit the season, this is a real DIY dinner party. The main course is an Oriental version of *moules marinière* served with Chinese noodles and a bowl of shiny crisp vegetables. The fragrant mussel broth is served piping hot as a light clear consommé for the first course. For dessert, sautéed pears or apples are piled on circles of golden puff pastry to make luscious tartlets. Nobody will guess the whole meal took around 45 minutes to put together – not unless you discreetly mention it.

CLEAR BROTH
WITH THAI SPICES

MUSSELS WITH
LEMON GRASS
AND NOODLES

CRISP VEGETABLE
MEDLEY

FOR 5

INSTANT FRUIT TART
OF THE SEASON

MUSSELS WITH LEMON GRASS AND NOODLES

M ost mussels on sale these days are already quite clean and require only a few minutes brushing. Alternatively, look in your supermarket for tubs of cleaned mussels or vacuum-packs of small Irish mussels.

1.5 litres/2¹/₂pt or 2¹/₂lb clean small fresh mussels

200ml/8fl oz dry white wine

1 sachet of Thai herbs and spices (i.e. a few sprigs of coriander, 1 stalk of lemon grass, 3 lime leaves, 1 or 2 chilli peppers)

soy sauce

4 spring onions

1 packet of medium Chinese egg noodles, preferably fresh (about 450g/1lb)

small bunch of chives

3 tbsp groundnut or sunflower oil

2 garlic cloves

4cm/1¹/₂in piece of fresh ginger

salt and pepper

1   Scrub the mussels under cold running water. Pull out and cut off the beards (discarding any mussels that stay open during this treatment). Pour the wine into a large heavy pan, add about 575ml/1pt water and place over a high heat.

2   Reserve 3 sprigs of coriander. Split open the lemon grass and tear the lime leaves. Remove the seeds from the chilli (scraping the insides with a sharp knife so as not to burn your fingers). Chop the spring onions, add the coriander, lemon grass, lime leaves and deseeded chilli to the water along with a tablespoon of soy sauce and half the spring onions. Cover and bring to a fast boil. As soon as the mixture bubbles, tip in the prepared mussels and cover again. Cook the mussels for 4–5 minutes, shaking the pan several times, until the shells open.

3   While the mussels are cooking, start to prepare the noodles. Bring plenty of water to the boil in a large wok or sauté pan, add a generous pinch of salt and 2 teaspoons of the oil.

4   Line a colander with a double layer of dampened muslin and place over a large bowl. Tip the mussels into the colander and leave until cool enough to handle. Reserve the strained liquid.

5   Discard the flavourings and any mussels that have not opened. Shell the rest, working over the colander and adding any juices to the cooking liquid. Reserve about 10 mussels on their half shell for serving. Keep all the mussels in a warm place until ready to serve.

FAST FLOW

1
Preheat oven, boil kettle of water

2
Scrub mussels, prepare broth

3
Stamp out pastry tartlets, bake and cool

4
Prepare and sauté fruit, keep warm

5
Cook mussels and prepare noodles

6
Drain mussels, then shell and keep warm

7
Keep broth warm

8
Prepare and cook vegetables, keep warm

9
Cook noodles, drain, keep warm

10
Serve broth

11
Stir-fry noodles and mussels, serve

12
Dress vegetables, toss and serve

13
Assemble tartlets just before serving

TO DRINK

The white wines of Alsace go well with both seafood and Oriental spices: look out for a delicate Riesling, a more opulent Pinot Gris or a frankly spicy Gewürztraminer. Stay with the white wine for dessert or serve a little Poire liqueur or apple brandy on ice.

6 Rinse out the pan and pour in the strained liquid. Adjust the seasoning, snip in a few of the reserved coriander leaves and a few chives. Keep the broth very hot. When ready to serve, pour into small individual bowls (preferably warmed), reserving a few tablespoons of the broth to moisten the noodles. Snip a few chives over each portion, garnish with a small coriander leaf or two and serve as a starter.

7 Cook the noodles in fast boiling water according to the instructions on the packet. Drain in a large colander.

8 Wipe the wok or sauté pan with paper towels. Smash, peel and finely chop the garlic. Peel and grate the ginger (you will need only about half the piece; the extra is to protect your fingers when grating). Replace the wok over a fairly high heat and add the rest of the oil. Add the garlic and ginger to the hot oil and stir until golden. Tip in the noodles, stir to coat, then add the shelled mussels. Toss gently.

9 Transfer the mussels and noodles to a warmed serving bowl or individual bowls, if preferred. Garnish with chives, the remaining coriander and the rest of the spring onions. Arrange the mussels in the half shells decoratively on top, moisten with the reserved broth and serve immediately.

CRISP VEGETABLE MEDLEY

The choice of vegetables in this dish is very flexible; use water chestnuts in place of asparagus or broad beans in place of peas, if preferred.

Mussels with Lemon Grass (see page 81)

350g/12oz broccoli
400g/14oz bok-choy
225g/8oz thin asparagus spears
   or 225g/8oz canned water
   chestnuts, drained
225g/8oz fresh or frozen peas
   and/or broad beans
125g/4oz mangetout or
   sugarsnap peas
2 tbsp sunflower, groundnut or
   grapeseed oil
2 tsp toasted sesame oil
1/2 lime or lemon
salt and pepper

1 Bring to the boil about 7.5cm/3in lightly salted water in a large heavy saucepan or sauté pan. Prepare the vegetables: cut the broccoli into florets, separate the bok-choy leaves and cut them crosswise into wide strips. Cut the water chestnuts (if using) into very thin slices. Add the peas and/or broad beans, the broccoli florets and the bok-choy to the boiling water and cook for about 1 minute.

2 Cut off and discard the tough end of the asparagus spears (if using). Add the tips to the pan along with the mangetout or sugarsnap peas and cook for 2–3 minutes until the vegetables are cooked but still crunchy.

3 Drain well. Tip into a warmed shallow serving bowl. Drizzle over the oil and sesame oil and grate over a little lime or lemon zest. Squeeze a few drops of juice over the vegetables, toss lightly and adjust the seasoning.

4 Arrange the vegetables as attractively as possible and serve immediately to accompany the mussels and noodles.

INSTANT FRUIT TART OF THE SEASON

B ought puff pastry is not made with butter and benefits enormously from the buttery juices of the sautéed pears or apples in this recipe. Use fresh chilled puff pastry rather than the frozen and defrosted variety: ready-rolled, it takes no time at all to prepare for baking. Apricots, plums, nectarines and peaches make other irresistible toppings. All but the apricots need to be cooked a little more gently and quickly than apples and pears.

about 225g/8oz chilled ready-rolled puff pastry

1 egg yolk mixed with a little milk, for glazing

4–5 ripe but firm pears or apples

2 tsp lemon juice

55g/2oz unsalted butter

4 tbsp caster sugar

pinch of ground cinnamon

2 tbsp Poire liqueur or apple brandy

vanilla ice cream or crème fraîche, to serve

1 Preheat the oven to 200°C/400°F/gas 6 and insert a baking tray. Using a 10cm/4in biscuit cutter or fluted tartlet tin, stamp out 4 pastry circles. Score a cross in the centre of each. If you like, use a smaller biscuit cutter to stamp out little crescents of leftover pastry. Brush all the pastry shapes lightly with the egg yolk and milk mixture.

2 Put the circles and crescents on the tray and bake for about 5 minutes. Remove the crescents, which should be a little puffed and golden, and return the tray with the circles to the oven.

3 Bake for another 3–4 minutes, until puffed up and golden. Set aside on a cooling rack until ready to use.

4 Peel the pears, quarter and remove the core. If using apples, simply core and cut into 4–8 segments.

5 Sprinkle the pears or apples with lemon juice. Melt half the butter over a moderate heat in a frying pan. Scatter half the caster sugar over the melted butter as evenly as possible. Stir for 2–3 minutes until golden.

6 Add the fruit to the pan, spreading it evenly. Sauté for 3 minutes over a moderate heat, shaking the pan a few times without stirring.

7 Turn over the fruit and reduce the heat a fraction. Cut the rest of the butter into small pieces and scatter them among the fruit. Sprinkle with the rest of the caster sugar and the cinnamon. Cook for 3–5 minutes until the fruit is golden, without shaking or stirring during the first 2 minutes. Cover and keep warm until needed.

8 Arrange the fruit attractively on the tartlets. Top the tartlets with the pastry crescents, if using, by tucking them in at an angle between the pieces of fruit. Serve the tartlets warm with a sprinkling of Poire liqueur and a scoop of vanilla ice cream or a generous helping of crème fraîche.

SUMMER AFTER-THEATRE SUPPER

Obviously, if you know you are going out to the theatre or cinema, you might choose to make the granita and the soup before you leave and put them to chill and freeze – you could also put the duck to marinate.

Even if you can't manage that degree of early preparation, however, this light and elegant meal is quick to make after you get back home from your evening's entertainment. If you're really stuck for time, just serve a good-quality vanilla ice cream for dessert, liberally sprinkled with the pistachio nuts and Grand Marnier.

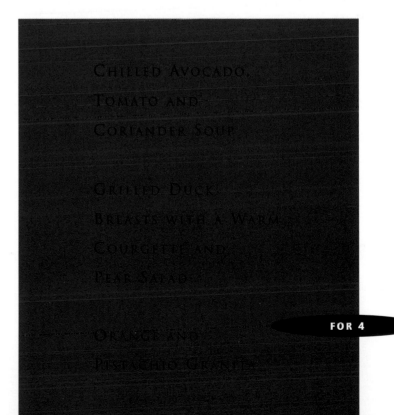

CHILLED AVOCADO,
TOMATO AND
CORIANDER SOUP

GRILLED DUCK
BREASTS WITH A WARM
COURGETTE AND
PEAR SALAD

ORANGE AND
PISTACHIO GRANITA

FOR 4

CHILLED AVOCADO, TOMATO AND CORIANDER SOUP

This delicious and refreshing chilled soup is based on the traditional Mexican avocado dip, guacamole. The soup has lots of flavour and punch made with just water, but tastes more rounded if a well-flavoured vegetable or chicken stock is used. Try to use ripe, black-skinned Hass avocados. If you leave out the tomatoes you can still make a very good soup with a sharp coriander flavour and a strikingly clear emerald colour.

400g/14oz canned chopped plum tomatoes

4 spring onions

2 limes

3 large ripe avocados

300ml/¹/₂pt water or good-quality vegetable or chicken stock

handful of coriander leaves

4–5 ice cubes

Tabasco sauce

salt and pepper

1 Pour the tomatoes into a sieve placed over a bowl and leave to drain off as much moisture as possible.

2 Coarsely chop the spring onions into the bowl of a food processor and add the juice of the limes, the flesh of 2 of the avocados, the water or stock, all but a few sprigs of the coriander and the ice cubes. Whizz to a purée.

3 Add the remaining avocado and all but a few spoonfuls of the drained tomato flesh and pulse until the flesh of the avocado is broken up but small chunks of it are still visible. Do not over-process. If necessary, adjust the consistency with a little more water or stock or by pulsing in some more ice cubes. Season generously to taste with salt, pepper and Tabasco sauce.

4 Pour the soup into individual serving bowls, spoon a little of the reserved chopped tomato into the centre of each bowl and top with a reserved coriander leaf.

TO DRINK

A fresh lively red like a Fleurie or a Californian Gamay-Beaujolais throughout the meal, with perhaps a small reinforcing glass of the orange liqueur with the granita.

Opposite: Chilled Avocado, Tomato and Coriander Soup

FAST FLOW

1 Turn freezer to coldest setting as far ahead as possible

2 Make granita and put to freeze

3 Prepare duck

4 Put tomatoes for soup to drain

5 Preheat grill and put on water to blanch courgettes and pears

6 Prepare watercress, pears and courgettes

7 Line plates with watercress and make salad dressing

8 Mix up granita and return to freezer with liqueur and serving glasses

9 Make soup and serve

10 Put duck to grill while eating soup (but be prepared to dodge back to the grill once or twice during that course)

11 While duck is resting after grilling: blanch courgette and pear strips, drain and arrange on plates

12 Slice duck and arrange on plates, dress and serve

13 Spoon granita into glasses, pour over liqueur and decorate with nuts

GRILLED DUCK BREASTS WITH A WARM COURGETTE AND PEAR SALAD

Conference pears are probably the best variety to use for this dish because they slice and cook well, keeping a good shape and texture. Roquefort would be a classic choice of blue cheese for the garnish, but you could also try the wonderful new blue British goats' cheese, Harbourne Blue, made by prize-winning cheese-maker Robin Congdon at Ticklemore Cheeses in Devon and now available at better delicatessens and food halls.

2 large duck breasts
1 tbsp Dijon mustard
2 tbsp clear honey
bunch of watercress
2 large ripe but firm dessert pears
4 courgettes
about 55g/2oz blue cheese

for the dressing:
2 tbsp walnut oil
3 tbsp sunflower oil
$^1/_4$ lemon
salt and pepper

1 Score the fatty side of the duck breasts across diagonally at about 1cm/$^1/_2$in intervals and deep enough to get through to the flesh beneath. This facilitates rapid cooking. Mix the mustard and some pepper into the honey and brush this all over the fatty sides of the breasts. Set aside.

2 Preheat the grill to high and put a large pan of lightly salted water to boil.

3 Trim, wash and pat dry the watercress, if necessary. Peel, quarter lengthwise and core the pears. Trim the ends of the courgettes. Using a vegetable peeler or cheese slicer, pare the courgettes lengthwise into long shavings. Slice the pear quarters thinly.

4 Grill the duck breasts, skin side up, for about 5 minutes, until the fat is well browned. Turn over and cook for about 2–3 minutes on the other side. This produces duck that is nicely browned on the outside but still fairly pink inside; if you prefer your duck well done, reduce the grill temperature to moderate and cook the breasts for a further 5–10 minutes on each side.

5 While the duck breasts are grilling, line each of the serving plates with a bed of watercress. Make the salad dressing by mixing the oils with the juice from the lemon quarter. Season with salt and pepper to taste.

6 Once the duck breasts are ready, remove from the grill and cover with foil. Leave in a warm place to settle for a few minutes.

7 While the duck is resting, drop the courgette and pear shavings into the pan of rapidly boiling water and blanch for just as long as it takes for the water to return to a good rolling boil. Immediately remove from the pan, drain well and pat dry on paper towels. Heap an attractive pile of courgette and pear shavings on one side of each dressed plate.

8 Using a sharp knife, cut each duck breast across at a slight angle into slices about 1cm/$^1/_2$in thick and fan these around the other side of each serving plate. Spoon the dressing over the salad and crumble a little blue cheese over the top to finish.

ORANGE AND PISTACHIO GRANITA

Any form of frozen dessert is a bit of a challenge for the fast cook. Here a couple of tricks are employed to speed the freezing process. It really helps to use a ready-made syrup rather than making your own, which would have to cool. Also, as alcohol in a mixture slows down freezing, the flavouring liqueur is not incorporated in the mixture but is instead chilled separately and used as a dressing.

In the time allowed the granita will probably be fairly slushy, but that is the optimum consistency – you don't want something rock-hard. You will need two standard-size ice trays for this recipe.

12–16 ice cubes
225ml/8fl oz good-quality orange juice
1/4 lemon
150ml/1/4pt golden syrup
55g/2oz unsalted pistachio nuts
3 tbsp Grand Marnier or other orange-flavoured liqueur

1 As far ahead as possible, turn the freezer to its coldest setting.

2 Put the ice cubes in the food processor with the orange juice and whizz until broken up into a slush.

3 Squeeze in the juice from the lemon, add the syrup and pistachios (reserving a few for decoration) and whizz until well mixed. The nuts should be chopped fairly finely but not to a powder.

4 Pour into chilled ice trays and put in the freezer for about 30 minutes. Take out and mix with a fork, then replace in the freezer for at least another 20 minutes. Put the liqueur and the serving glasses or bowls to chill.

5 Just before serving, remove the granita from the freezer. It will probably be fairly soft, so just spoon it into the glasses or bowls; if it is quite hard, pop the cubes back into the processor and pulse briefly to break them up to a spoonable consistency.

6 Pour the chilled liqueur over and decorate with the reserved nuts.

CHICKEN LIVERS WITH BACON AND TOMATOES ON PASTA

Inexpensive chicken livers make a superb, gutsy pasta sauce. They are usually sold frozen, so allow plenty of time to defrost them. While fresh pasta is quicker to cook, the dried spirals chosen here work out a lot cheaper.

350–450g/12–16oz dried pasta spirals
1 onion
1 garlic clove
8 rashers of smoked streaky bacon
3 sprigs of fresh rosemary
225g/8oz chicken livers
2 tbsp olive oil
400g/14oz canned tomatoes
1 tsp balsamic vinegar
salt and pepper

1 Boil the water for the pasta and cook it according to the packet instructions.

2 Chop the onion, garlic, bacon and 2 sprigs of rosemary. Trim the chicken livers with a sharp knife by removing any connective tissue, and coarsely slice them. Wash and pat dry.

3 Heat the oil in a pan. Sauté the onion with the garlic for a couple of minutes over a medium heat. Add the bacon and sauté for a further minute, then add the trimmed chicken livers. Drain the tomatoes, tip them into the pan, mashing them gently to break them up slightly, then add the chopped rosemary. Cook for 3–4 minutes, or until the livers are just cooked, but still pink.

4 Adjust the seasoning and stir in the balsamic vinegar. Tip into the cooked pasta and snip over some of the reserved rosemary.

HOT APPLES IN CIDER

The variety of apple you use will depend on what is in season. Look out for firm, well-textured fruit with bags of flavour such as the early Discovery or, later on in the season, Russet or Cox.

4 dessert apples
55g/2oz unsalted butter
55g/2oz brown sugar
100ml/3^{1}/2fl oz dry cider
squeeze of lemon juice
1 tsp ground cinnamon

1 Core and quarter the apples and cut into slices about 1cm/^{1}/2in thick.

2 Melt the butter in a pan. Add the apples and the sugar and stir carefully until they are thoroughly coated. Fry gently over a medium to low heat for about 4 minutes, until the apples are tender but still retain their texture. Lift the apples out of the pan using a slotted spoon. Arrange on a serving dish and keep warm.

3 Turn up the heat, add the cider and deglaze the pan. Continue stirring until the liquid reduces to a thick syrup, then add the squeeze of lemon juice.

4 Pour the sauce over the apples, sprinkle over the cinnamon and serve.

Hot Apples in Cider

WATERCRESS, ORANGE AND RADISH SALADE MAROCAINE

The refreshingly sharp taste of radishes and watercress make this salad the pefect complement to the rich Aubergine Tian. Thinly sliced chicory is a possible addition, as are toasted slivered almonds.

bunch or sachet of fresh firm radishes (discard any bruised ones)
large sachet or about 125g/4^1/$_2$ oz ready-washed watercress
1^1/$_2$ ripe oranges
1 small lemon
2^1/$_2$ tbsp olive oil
12 small black olives (optional)
salt and pepper

1 Wash the radishes, trim if necessary and pat dry with paper towels. Cut the larger ones into rings. Cut off and discard the thicker watercress stalks.

2 Skin the whole orange, remove as much white pith as possible, thinly slice and discard the pips. Grate the zest and squeeze out the juice from the remaining half orange, then squeeze the lemon.

3 In a cup, combine the orange zest and juice, the lemon juice, olive oil, a pinch of salt and a sprinkling of pepper.

4 Put the watercress and radishes in a wide shallow bowl. Drizzle over the dressing, reserving 1 tablespoon. Toss lightly. Adjust the seasoning.

5 Distribute the orange slices over the salad. Scatter over the black olives, if using. Drizzle over the rest of the dressing and serve as soon as possible.

TO DRINK

Either a light and fruity new-season red (young Beaujolais or nuovo vintage Italian) or a full-bodied white wine (New World Chardonnay) with the main course. With the dessert, try a fortified wine: Oloroso sherry, Madeira, port or Vin Santo.

Watercress, Orange and Radish Salade Marocaine

CHICKEN BREASTS WITH CUCUMBER AND TARRAGON SAUCE

Most people rarely think of cooking with lettuce, yet it produces a delicate pale green sauce, tinged with lemony sharpness. The sweeter the lettuce, the sweeter the sauce, which is why baby Little Gems work best.

4 boned chicken breasts
1 cucumber
2 Little Gem or 1 cos lettuce(s)
handful of fresh tarragon
30g/1oz butter
300ml/1/2 pint chicken stock
3 tbsp dry white wine
salt and pepper

1 Skin the chicken breasts and slice them in two lengthwise. Peel and coarsely chop the cucumber. Roughly shred the lettuce, discarding any outer leaves. Chop about 8 tarragon leaves.

2 Melt the butter in a pan over a medium heat. Add the cucumber and lettuce and toss in the butter until thoroughly coated. Pour over the chicken stock and white wine and add the tarragon leaves. Raise the heat and bring to a simmer.

3 Place the chicken breasts on top of the cucumber mixture. Cover, reduce the heat and gently poach the chicken for 7–10 minutes, until cooked through. Remove from the pan and keep warm.

4 Transfer the cucumber mixture to a food processor. Whizz to a rough purée.

5 Adjust the seasoning. Pour the sauce into a shallow serving dish, arrange the chicken on top and decorate with tarragon leaves.

SUMMER BERRY BRÛLÉE

320g/11oz caster sugar
350g/12oz raspberries, strawberries and blueberries, or a selection of berries of your choice
1 orange
200ml/7fl oz crème fraîche

1 Dampen 4 ramekins with water, then swill 20g/1/2 oz of sugar around them so it sticks to the edges.

2 Halve or quarter any large strawberries. In a bowl, mix the berries together. Squeeze half the orange and sprinkle the juice over the berries, then spoon them into the ramekins.

3 Grate the whole orange and mix the zest into the cream. Spread thickly over the berries. Chill in the refrigerator.

4 Melt the remaining sugar in a saucepan over a moderate heat, turning the saucepan to ensure the sugar melts evenly. (Watch it carefully – if it catches it can burn very quickly.) When the sugar has turned a rich caramel brown, quickly remove the pan from the heat on to a heat-proof surface, taking great care as the sugar will continue to heat in the pan. Pour the melted sugar immediately over the crème fraîche to form an even layer. Leave in a cool place (not the refrigerator) to harden.

Warm Salmon Salad (see page 105)

Special
occasions

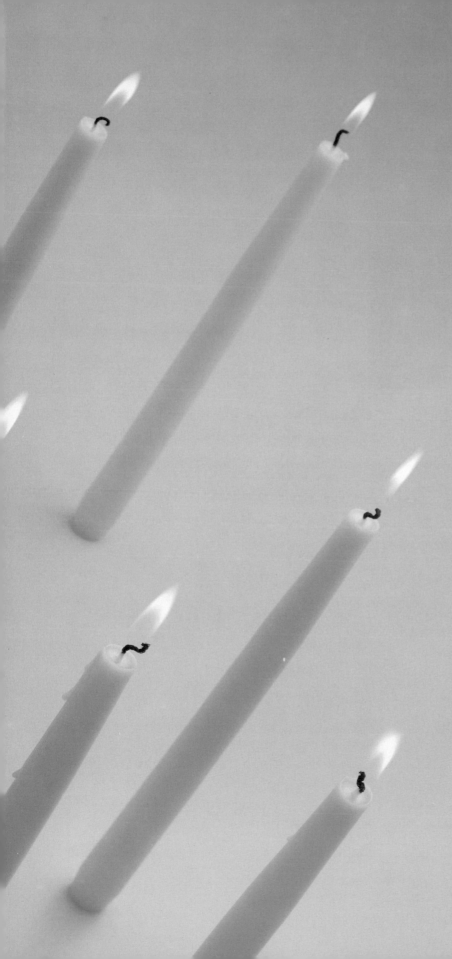

BIRTHDAY PARTY
- CELEBRATION BURGERS WITH ASSORTED SALSAS
- PACIFIC RIM SALAD
- CHOCOLATE AND AMARETTI TRUFFLE CAKE

VALENTINE DÎNER À DEUX
- OYSTERS AND CAVIAR
- GRILLED FILLET STEAKS WITH DEVILLED
  MUSHROOM SAUCE
- NEW POTATOES WITH ARTICHOKE HEARTS
- INSTANT STRAWBERRY SHORTCAKES

ANNIVERSARY DINNER
- SAUTÉED FOIE GRAS WITH SAUTERNES-SOAKED
  SULTANAS
- SCALLOP WALDORF TIÈDE
- ATHOLL BROSE

CONGRATULATIONS PARTY
- MUSHROOM AND CHEESE CROUSTADES
- ROAST HALIBUT WITH CAPERS AND PARSLEY
- VANILLA ICE CREAM WITH CRANBERRY AND
  COINTREAU COULIS

LAST-MINUTE CHRISTMAS
RECIPES
- SMOKY ANGELS AND DEVILS
- POTTED CHEESE
- SMOKED SALMON OMELETTE SOUFFLÉ
- PARSNIP, CELERIAC AND POTATO GRATIN
- BRAISED RED CABBAGE WITH TANGERINES
- CHRISTMAS CLUB SANDWICH
- TURKEY FRICASSÉE
- TURKEY BROTH
- CHRISTMAS PUDDING ICE CREAM

BIRTHDAY PARTY

Generally for occasions like family birthdays and anniversaries you do have a chance to prepare ahead. Every so often, however, with the best will in the world you simply don't have the time – or, let's face it, you just forget. Nevertheless it's still possible to conjure up a fairly impressive meal in a matter of minutes, which will look as if you've been planning it secretly for weeks. An added bonus is that the birthday cake – a rich combination of chocolate and almond flavours – requires no baking at all.

CELEBRATION BURGERS
WITH ASSORTED SALSAS

PACIFIC RIM SALAD

CHOCOLATE AND
AMARETTI TRUFFLE
CAKE

FOR 6–8

CELEBRATION BURGERS WITH ASSORTED SALSAS

Grilled hamburgers are perfect family fare. These are filled with a very sophisticated anchovy and goats' cheese stuffing which turns them into surprise packages and gives them a more upmarket appeal. The fresh and spicy sweetcorn and tomato salsas also help elevate these icons of fast food into the gourmet class.

1.35kg/3lb best (low-fat) minced steak
2 red onions, plus extra to serve (optional)
large handful of flat-leaf parsley
several dashes of Worcestershire sauce
2 eggs
170g/6oz mushrooms
1 small log of goats' cheese
12 canned anchovies
salt and pepper

for the sweetcorn salsa:
170g/6oz frozen sweetcorn kernels
1/2 cucumber
1 yellow pepper
3–4 spring onions
small handful of coriander
1 lime
1/2 tbsp honey
1 small yellow or green chilli pepper

for the tomato salsa:
6 large ripe but firm tomatoes, preferably plum
1 red onion
1 red pepper
small handful of parsley

1 lemon
pinch of brown sugar
1/2 tsp Dijon mustard
dash of sherry vinegar or red wine vinegar
1 small red chilli pepper

1 As far ahead as possible, take the sweetcorn for the salsa out of the freezer and arrange on a large flat plate to defrost. Then put the mince for the burgers in a large bowl. Chop the onions and add them to the bowl, then snip in the parsley. Season and add one or two dashes of Worcestershire sauce. Beat the eggs lightly in a small bowl and stir into the mixture. Mix everything well with the fingers. Leave to marinate for as long as possible.

2 Make the salsas: for the sweetcorn salsa, dice the cucumber into a bowl, deseed and dice the yellow pepper and add to the bowl. Snip in the spring onions and coriander. Squeeze in the lime juice and add the honey, the sweetcorn and some salt and pepper. For the tomato salsa, halve the tomatoes, scoop out and discard the seeds and then dice the flesh. Put in

FAST FLOW

❶ Put cream and eggs for cake to chill and put cake tin in freezer
❷ Defrost sweetcorn for salsa if necessary
❸ Prepare burger mixture and leave to marinate
❹ Make cake and put to freeze
❺ Make salsas
❻ Make salad and dressing
❼ Preheat a hot grill for burgers
❽ Prepare mushrooms, stir into burger mix and prepare burgers
❾ Cook burgers
❿ Dry-fry almonds and finish salad
⓫ Serve burgers with salsas and salad
⓬ Unmould and decorate cake

TO DRINK

With the savouries, you might opt for beer in the presence of so much lime juice, chilli and other pungent flavours, or try a good Californian red. After beer, try some good coffee with the cake, or a not-too-dry sparkling wine to mark the occasion.

another bowl. Coarsely chop the onion, then deseed and dice the red pepper and add to the tomato. Snip in the parsley. Squeeze in the lemon juice and add the sugar, mustard, vinegar and some salt and pepper. Finally, deseed and finely chop the chillies and add them to the respective salsas. Stir both salsas well.

3 When ready to cook the hamburgers, preheat a hot grill, ridged grilling pan or barbecue. Chop the mushrooms fairly finely and stir these into the meat mixture. Mix well again with the fingers. Take out little golf-ball-sized lumps of the mixture, roll into balls and flatten to thin discs (aim for about 24 balls to give you 12 burgers – 2 each for 6 people and $1\frac{1}{2}$ each for 8). Lay these out on a work surface.

4 Slice the cheese into discs about 3mm/$\frac{1}{8}$in thick and lay a slice of cheese on 12 of the burger discs. Put a drained anchovy fillet on top of each cheese slice. Place an uncoated burger disc on top of each of the coated ones as if you are making sandwiches and pinch lightly but carefully round the edges to seal.

5 When the grill, grilling pan or barbecue is good and hot, cook the hamburgers until they are well browned on each side. Exact timing will depend on the equipment you are using and how well done you like your burgers to be.

6 Serve the burgers with the bowls of sweetcorn and tomato salsa and some chopped red onion, if using.

PACIFIC RIM SALAD

The flavours of California and the Orient are combined here to produce an extremely refreshing yet unusually satisfying salad which will appeal to even the most entrenched 'rabbit food' hater.

1 large head of bok-choy

170g/6oz beansprouts

115g/4oz seedless raisins

4 large juicy oranges

115g/4oz flaked almonds

for the chive yogurt dressing:

3–4 tbsp sherry vinegar

300ml/$\frac{1}{2}$ pt natural live yogurt

bunch of chives

salt and pepper

1 Shred the bok-choy into a large bowl. Add the beansprouts and all but a small handful of the raisins.

2 Peel the oranges and slice them thickly, then cut the slices into quarters. Add all but a handful to the salad bowl and mix well.

3 Make the dressing: mix the vinegar into the yogurt and season to taste.

4 Just before serving, dry-fry the almonds briefly over a low-to-moderate heat until just brown, tossing all the time – be careful not to let them burn. Set aside off the heat.

5 Snip the chives into the dressing and pour it over the salad. Sprinkle over the reserved raisins and orange segments and finish by sprinkling the toasted almonds over the top.

Chocolate and Amaretti Truffle Cake (see page 114)

CHOCOLATE AND AMARETTI TRUFFLE CAKE

Nothing gives a sense of occasion like a chocolate cake. This refrigerator cake looks good and is full of flavour – and as it's so rich it will go a long way. As the cake is uncooked, use only the freshest eggs.

4 tbsp crème fraîche or double cream
2 very fresh eggs
250g/8¹/₂oz good-quality plain chocolate
85g/3oz butter
2 tbsp Cointreau
200g/7oz amaretti biscuits
55g/2oz stem ginger
birthday cake candles and sugared almonds to decorate (optional)

1 As far ahead as possible turn the refrigerator and freezer to their highest setting. Chill the cream and eggs in the refrigerator and put a 20cm/8in cake tin in the freezer.

2 Break three-quarters of the chocolate into a bowl set over a pan of barely simmering water to melt. Put the rest of the chocolate in the refrigerator.

3 Meanwhile, heat the butter in a small pan or in the microwave until just melted. Separate the eggs and beat the whites until standing in soft peaks. In another bowl, beat the cream until it stands in soft peaks.

4 As soon as the chocolate has melted, stand the bowl in cold water and stir in the egg yolks, melted butter and Cointreau. Mix well. Add the cream and a little of the egg whites and stir them in well. Then add the rest of the egg whites and fold in gently.

5 Dot the base of the chilled cake tin with biscuits until almost covered, leaving a clear space around the edge. Break the remaining biscuits into 2 or 3 pieces into the chocolate mixture. Coarsely chop the ginger and add to the chocolate. Stir in gently and pour the mixture into the cake tin. Level the surface and return to the freezer for as long as possible (at least 45 minutes).

6 Just before serving, remove the cake tin from the freezer and dip it briefly in hot water to unmould. Decorate with the reserved chocolate grated over the top. Add the birthday candles, if using, and pick out the celebrant's name in sugared almonds.

VALENTINE DÎNER À DEUX

The purpose of this meal is to create a magical atmosphere that is at once gently romantic and intensely seductive. This seemingly madly indulgent assemblage of luxurious tastes and sensuous textures will work wonders, inflaming passions for new *amours* and long-standing couples alike.

As the two of you want to spend as much time together at the table as possible, it is best to get all four dishes almost ready before eating and keep them warm (or cold, as appropriate).

OYSTERS AND CAVIAR

GRILLED FILLET STEAKS
WITH DEVILLED
MUSHROOM SAUCE

NEW POTATOES WITH
ARTICHOKE HEARTS

FOR 2

INSTANT STRAWBERRY
SHORTCAKES

OYSTERS AND CAVIAR

At the prices you will be paying (a dozen oysters will cost you as much as a bottle of supermarket champagne), good fishmongers will clean and prepare the oysters for you – many local suppliers will even deliver them ready for the table, carefully packed in ice – and they can be safely opened a few hours before serving as long as they are kept refrigerated in their shells.

If you have to prepare them yourself, scrub them well under cold running water, then to open each oyster put it, curved shell down, in a clean, dry tea towel in your left hand (or in your right, if you are left-handed), with the hinge facing away from you. Insert an oyster knife or very stout short knife into the hinge and work it back and forth to prise the shells apart. Being very careful to keep the oyster level so as not to lose any of the juices, remove and discard the top (flat) shell. Wipe the knife clean on your towel and then run it under the oyster meat to cut it free of the curved shell.

Again, having splashed out on your oysters, it would be a pity to spoil this dish with a poor-quality lumpfish roe; go the extra distance with a tiny tin of caviar or at least salmon or trout eggs – after all, you are proving your love. If you use half dark caviar or roe and half red salmon or trout eggs, you can create a very attractive effect indeed.

1 dozen native oysters
4 tbsp caviar or salmon or trout
  eggs
cayenne pepper
lemon wedges, to serve
watercress or seaweed, to garnish
  (optional)

1 Arrange the oysters in their curved shells on an indented oyster plate or nestle them into a pile of coarse sea salt mounded on a serving plate.

2 Garnish the plates with lemon wedges and with watercress or seaweed, if using.

3 Sprinkle a teaspoonful of caviar or fish eggs over each oyster and dust very lightly with cayenne pepper.

TO DRINK

A half bottle of good Chablis with the oysters, another of St Émilion with the steaks and a glass of sweet Vouvray for the strawberries – or the best pink champagne throughout the meal.

FAST FLOW

1 Remove steaks from refrigerator well ahead of cooking

2 Prepare strawberries and toss in sugar as early as possible

3 Put potatoes to boil or steam

4 Preheat grill or ridged grilling pan

5 Prepare oysters and arrange on plates (but do not dress with the caviar or roe)

6 Whip cream for strawberries and keep in refrigerator

7 Grill steaks

8 Make sauce while steaks are grilling

9 Drain and finish potatoes; keep warm

10 Plate steaks and their sauce, cover and keep warm in a low oven

11 Put scones to warm in the oven

12 Finish and serve oysters

13 Serve steaks and potatoes

14 Assemble and serve strawberry shortcakes

GRILLED FILLET STEAKS WITH DEVILLED MUSHROOM SAUCE

These steaks can be grilled in the conventional way, but we recommend using a heavy ridged grilling pan placed over a very high heat on the hob. The searing contact heat gives you more of the effect you get from the very intense grills that restaurants tend to have – and produces an attractive striped effect on the surface of the steaks.

Use a mixture of predominantly ordinary button mushrooms with any wild mushrooms you can lay your hands on. If there are no fresh wild mushrooms available, use oyster mushrooms and/or shiitake.

225g/8oz assorted mushrooms (see above)

2 fillet steaks, each weighing about 225g/8oz

45g/1¹/₂oz butter

1 tbsp olive oil, plus extra for greasing

3 spring onions, plus extra to garnish (optional)

1 tbsp balsamic vinegar, sherry vinegar or best-quality red wine vinegar

100ml/3¹/₂fl oz red wine

dash of Worcestershire sauce

dash of Tabasco sauce

salt and pepper

1 Preheat the grill to high or place the grilling pan over a high heat. Wipe and thinly slice the button mushrooms. Pick over the wild, oyster or shiitake mushrooms and slice if large.

2 Brush the grill lightly with oil and put the steaks to grill to the required degree (about 2 minutes on each side for very rare, to 5 minutes on each side for well done).

3 While they are grilling, make the sauce: melt half the butter with the oil in a sauté pan. Snip in the spring onions and sauté for a minute or so over a medium heat until just beginning to soften.

4 Add the button mushrooms, increase the heat slightly and sauté for 2–3 minutes, until just softening.

5 Add any wild, oyster or shiitake mushrooms to the pan with the vinegar and cook for 1–2 minutes more, until the mushrooms are soft and dark.

6 Add the wine, Worcestershire sauce, Tabasco and salt and pepper to taste. Stir well over a high heat for a minute or so to deglaze the pan, then stir in the remaining butter.

7 Put the steaks on serving plates and spoon the sauce over. Garnish by snipping over some more spring onion greens, if using.

If Time Allows

Substitute some dried sliced mushrooms, like ceps (porcini) for the wild mushrooms. Use about 30g/1oz, rinse well and soak for about 30 minutes in the wine.

NEW POTATOES WITH ARTICHOKE HEARTS

One of the helpful revolutions in our supermarkets in recent years has been the presence of those punnets of tasty little 'designer' new potatoes almost all year round. These usually need virtually no preparation.

225g/8oz small new potatoes
30g/1oz butter
**225g/8oz canned artichoke
    hearts**
1/2 lemon
few chive stalks
handful of parsley
salt and pepper

1 Boil the potatoes until they are tender but still have a bit of bite (from 10–20 minutes, depending on variety and size). Drain, return to the pan and dry over a low heat.

2 Add the butter and the drained artichokes to the pan. Toss gently over a low heat to mix and coat the vegetables well with the butter.

3 Transfer to a warmed serving dish and squeeze over a little lemon juice.

4 Season well and snip over the chives and parsley.

INSTANT STRAWBERRY SHORTCAKES

170g/6oz strawberries
3 tbsp sugar
**2 large good-quality freshly baked
    scones**
150ml/1/4pt double cream
**1 tbsp (or extra to taste) Grand
    Marnier or other orange-
    flavoured liqueur**
20g/1/2oz butter

1 Wash and hull the strawberries, dry them well with paper towels and slice thickly lengthwise.

2 In a bowl, gently toss the strawberry slices in the sugar and set aside for as long as possible.

3 Put the scones on a baking tray and put to warm in a low oven.

4 In a second bowl, whip the cream with the liqueur until the cream is standing in soft peaks.

5 Remove the warmed scones from the oven, split each in half widthwise and spread the two bottom halves with the butter.

6 Arrange a thick layer of strawberry slices on top of each buttered scone half. Cover generously with cream.

7 Put the two unbuttered scone halves on top, cover with another thick layer of cream, strawberry slices and more cream (if there is any left).

8 Arrange any remaining strawberry slices decoratively around the shortcakes and serve immediately.

If Time Allows

Cut out a paper heart smaller than the scone, place it on the top layer of strawberries and dust with icing sugar from a sieve. Lift away the paper to reveal a brilliant crimson heart.

Instant Strawberry Shortcakes

ANNIVERSARY DINNER

Anniversaries should be occasions when you get the chance to celebrate each other, so make this menu together, perhaps cooking alternate courses. You also want simple and fairly exquisite food involving the minimum of preparation and fuss, but clearly marking it out as a meal to remember. Here the traditional roles of fish and meat are reversed, with a starter of foie gras and a seafood main course, and the whole effect is one of lightness and delicacy. For the Atholl Brose recipe, see page 141.

For the Atholl Brose recipe, see page 141.

TO DRINK

The rest of the half bottle of Sauternes with the foie gras, followed by a fresh light white wine such as a Pouilly-Fuissé or an Alsace Sylvaner to combat the lime vinaigrette. Serve Drambuie with the pudding if you have room for more alcohol!

SAUTÉED FOIE GRAS
WITH SAUTERNES-
SOAKED SULTANAS

SCALLOP
WALDORF TIÈDE

ATHOLL BROSE

FOR 2

SAUTÉED FOIE GRAS WITH SAUTERNES-SOAKED SULTANAS

This truly sublime dish is based on one believed to have originated at Paris's famed Jamin restaurant, back in the days before master-chef Jöel Robuchon pioneered from there the swing away from *nouvelle cuisine* and the return to traditional *cuisine grand'mère*.

2 heaped tbsp sultanas
3 tbsp Sauternes
2 thick slices of fresh duck or goose foie gras, each weighing about 55g/2oz
1 tbsp cognac
30g/1oz butter
2 thick slices of brioche
3 tbsp good-quality chicken stock or canned consommé
flour, for dusting

1 Put the sultanas in a small pan and pour over the Sauternes. Leave to plump up for 10 minutes or so.

2 Meanwhile, put the slices of foie gras on a plate, sprinkle with the cognac and leave to marinate while the sultanas plump.

3 Bring the pan of plumped sultanas gently to a simmer.

4 While the sultanas are simmering, carefully transfer the foie gras (leaving any juices behind on the plate) to another plate. Dust very lightly on both sides with flour.

5 Melt two-thirds of the butter in a small frying pan over a moderate heat and then fry the foie gras slices for about 2–3 minutes on each side until just browned.

6 While the foie gras is cooking, toast the brioche slices lightly and arrange on two serving plates.

7 Arrange the cooked foie gras slices on the toasts.

8 Pour off the excess fat from the frying pan and pour in the stock, together with any cognac from the marinating plate. Deglaze the pan, stirring and scraping well. Stir in the sultanas and wine and bubble for a few minutes. Stir in the remaining butter to gloss the sauce.

9 Pour over the foie gras and serve.

FAST FLOW

❶
Put cream for Atholl Brose to chill in freezer

❷
Put sultanas to plump and marinate foie gras

❸
Make Atholl Brose and put to chill

❹
Dry-fry bacon for salad and prepare vegetables

❺
Make salad dressing

❻
Make salad, toss in dressing and arrange on plates

❼
Bring sultanas to simmer

❽
Dust foie gras and fry

❾
Toast brioche slices and arrange foie gras on them

❿
Deglaze foie gras pan and finish sauce

⓫
Finish foie gras and serve

⓬
Prepare and fry scallops

⓭
Finish salad and serve

SCALLOP WALDORF TIÈDE

S callops can reach extortionate prices, so splitting them across in two makes them go further as well as helping them cook quickly before they have a chance to go rubbery.

2–3 rashers of streaky bacon
¹/₂ green sweet pepper
¹/₂ red sweet pepper
2 celery stalks
3–4 spring onions
1 small sachet of ready-washed
    salad leaves (choose a crisp and
    colourful mix)
55g/2oz seedless muscat grapes
1 large ripe Anjou pear
5 large scallops (or more if the
    budget stretches)
30g/1oz walnut halves

for the lime cream vinaigrette:
¹/₂ lime
5 tbsp sunflower oil
1 tbsp crème fraîche
salt and pepper

1   Slice the bacon into small strips and dry-fry in a small non-stick frying pan until crisp. Remove from the pan and drain on paper towels. Leave any fat from the bacon in the pan.

2   Deseed the peppers and slice. Cut the celery into chunks and snip the spring onions as finely as possible.

3   To make the vinaigrette, squeeze the juice of the lime into the oil, stir in the crème fraîche and season to taste. Mix well until emulsified.

4   Put the salad leaves, bacon and prepared vegetables in a salad bowl. Add all but a large handful of the grapes. Peel and core the pear. Cut into thick slices and add to the salad. Mix the dressing well again, pour over the salad and toss to coat evenly. Arrange the dressed salad on serving plates.

5   Put the frying pan (complete with any reserved bacon fat) over a high heat until good and hot. Meanwhile, cut each scallop across into 2 flat discs. Reserve whole any pink coral. Reduce the heat to moderate and fry the scallop halves and any pieces of coral for about 30 seconds on each side – on no account allow them to overcook.

6   Scatter the cooked scallops over the salad. Dot with the remaining grapes and the walnuts. Serve immediately.

If Time Allows
Make a large handful of garlic croutons (see page 142) and sprinkle these over the finished salad for extra crunch.

CONGRATULATIONS
PARTY

This substantial meal is designed to indulge and spoil the person for whom you are preparing it. If you want to serve a salad, try lamb's lettuce or watercress, sprinkled with a little walnut oil or olive oil. Season the salad lightly and chill it while you eat the first course and the fish. It will refresh the palate – as will the sharp cranberry coulis served for dessert. The tartness of the coulis works best with the creamiest and most luxurious of bought vanilla ice creams – inferior varieties need not apply.

MUSHROOM AND
CHEESE CROUSTADES

ROAST HALIBUT WITH
CAPERS AND PARSLEY

FOR 2

VANILLA ICE CREAM
WITH CRANBERRY AND
COINTREAU COULIS

MUSHROOM AND CHEESE CROUSTADES

The soft sweetness of brioche makes it a good base for the juicy mushroom preparation. Chilled brioche that has spent a day or two in the refrigerator is easier to cut and has an excellent texture for grilling.

**about 225g/8oz mixed
  mushrooms, such as button,
  oyster and chanterelle**
**1¹/₂ tbsp groundnut, sunflower or
  light-flavoured olive oil**
1 tsp balsamic vinegar
4 slices of slightly stale brioche
30g/1oz butter, softened
**30g/1oz blue cheese, such as
  Gorgonzola or Cashel Blue**
30g/1oz mature goats' cheese
handful of rocket or sorrel leaves
salt and pepper

1 Preheat the grill to high. Wipe the mushrooms. Prepare as appropriate: thinly slice button or cup mushrooms, tear up oyster mushrooms and leave small chanterelles intact.

2 Heat the oil in a large sauté or frying pan. Scatter in the mushrooms, season with a little salt and sauté for 3-4 minutes over a fairly high heat until just cooked and faintly golden in colour. Stir the mushrooms from time to time during cooking.

3 Sprinkle with the balsamic vinegar and stir. Drain well on a plate lined with a double layer of paper towels.

4 Meanwhile, toast one side of the brioche slices. Lightly butter the untoasted sides.

5 Arrange the mushrooms on the buttered brioche. Season with a little salt and pepper. Cut the cheeses into slivers. Put the blue cheese slivers over 2 mushroom brioches and the goats' cheese over the other two. Grill until the cheese is bubbling.

6 While the brioches are under the grill, arrange the rocket or sorrel leaves on two plates.

7 Put a blue cheese and a goats' cheese mushroom croustade on each plate. Season with a little extra pepper and serve immediately.

TO DRINK

A little champagne is called for before the meal and perhaps with the first course. With the fish, drink a New Zealand Chardonnay.

FAST FLOW

1
Chill wine

2
Preheat oven and heat water for potatoes

3
Prepare and boil potatoes

4
Sauté and drain mushrooms, toast brioches on one side

5
Prepare cranberry coulis

6
Dress and chill salad, if serving

7
Preheat grill, assemble mushroom croustades

8
Cook spring onion, parsley and capers. Season halibut

9
Put vanilla ice cream to soften

10
Roast halibut and finish off dish between courses

11
Grill and serve croustades

12
Reheat cranberry sauce before serving (optional)

ROAST HALIBUT WITH CAPERS AND PARSLEY

The gutsy combination of capers, parsley and anchovy works well with firm-textured fish such as the dependable halibut. Take care not to overcook the fish and dry it out. Once it is in the oven, it really should be served within about 10 minutes.

2 skinned halibut fillets, each weighing about 170g/6oz
2 spring onions
4–6 sprigs of flat-leaf parsley
4 anchovy fillets, drained
30g/1oz butter
2 tsp groundnut or sunflower oil
1 scant tbsp drained capers
6 tbsp dry white wine
4 tbsp single cream
salt and pepper

1 Preheat the oven to 220°C/425°F/gas 7. Season the fish with a little salt and a generous sprinkling of pepper. Cut or snip both white and green parts of the spring onions into thin slices. Snip the parsley, reserving a few leaves for garnish. Finely chop the anchovies.

2 Put a flameproof roasting pan over a moderate heat. Melt half the butter with the oil, then add the capers, the spring onions and snipped parsley. Cook for 2 minutes to soften, then moisten with half the wine and shake the pan.

3 Take the roasting pan off the heat. Lay the fish in it on top of the onion, parsley and caper mixture. Scatter over the anchovies and smear with the rest of the butter. Cover the roasting pan loosely with foil.

4 Bake for 6–8 minutes or until the fish is just cooked and flakes a little when prodded gently with a fork. Lift the fish from the pan and keep warm on two warmed serving plates.

5 Replace the pan over a moderate heat. Add the remaining wine, bring to a fast simmer and stir for a few seconds. Whisk in the cream.

6 Spoon the contents of the pan over the fish. Scatter over the reserved parsley and serve as soon as possible.

CRANBERRY AND COINTREAU COULIS

Roast Halibut with Capers and Parsley

about 350g/12oz cranberries, fresh or frozen
3–4 tbsp caster sugar
2 tbsp Cointreau
icing sugar, to taste
vanilla ice cream, to serve

1 Put the berries and the caster sugar in a saucepan. Add 6 tablespoons of water and bring to a simmer over a moderate heat.

2 Stir the contents of the pan for a few minutes until the cranberries pop and burst.

3 Take off the heat and leave to cool. Process the cooled mixture for a few seconds in a food processor.

4 Push the purée through a sieve into a bowl. Stir in the Cointreau. Adjust the sweetness with icing sugar. Reheat before serving with vanilla ice cream.

LAST-MINUTE CHRISTMAS RECIPES

Despite all the usual forward planning, the festive season often demands quick thinking on the kitchen front. Sometimes you have unexpected guests to cater for. Another time something overcooked or undefrosted means you have to make an eleventh-hour substitution. Or perhaps you simply want to use up leftovers to make a dish which will tempt jaded palates. To prepare you for every eventuality, the recipes in this section range from main-course dishes for the family, to party snacks for ten or so guests and supper dishes for two (see individual recipes for serving quantities).

SMOKY ANGELS AND DEVILS

POTTED CHEESE

SMOKED SALMON OMELETTE SOUFFLÉ

PARSNIP, CELERIAC AND POTATO GRATIN

BRAISED RED CABBAGE WITH TANGERINES

CHRISTMAS CLUB SANDWICH

TURKEY FRICASSÉE

TURKEY BROTH

CHRISTMAS PUDDING ICE CREAM

FOR 2–10

SMOKY ANGELS AND DEVILS

As well as rounding off a meal stylishly, these little rolls make perfect snacks with drinks. The intensity of the smoked oyster flavour is nicely counterpointed by the sweetness of the prunes.

MAKES 48

125g/4^1/2oz canned smoked
 oysters
250g/8^1/2oz ready-to-eat stoned
 prunes
12 thin rashers of rindless back
 bacon
black pepper
cayenne pepper

1 Preheat a hot grill. Soak some wooden cocktail sticks in water to prevent them scorching during cooking.

2 Drain the oysters and leave to drain further on paper towels. Cut the prunes in half if large (they should ideally be about the same size as the oysters or just slightly larger).

3 Cut the bacon rashers in half lengthwise and then cut each of the resulting strips across in half. (It is usually quickest to do this with all the rashers layered together.)

4 Place an oyster in the centre of half the bacon strips and a piece of prune in the centre of the rest. Season with black and cayenne pepper. Roll each strip of bacon up around its filling and secure in place with a drained cocktail stick.

5 Arrange the rolls on a grill pan and grill for about 10 minutes, turning over halfway through cooking, until the bacon is well browned.

6 Serve hot or warm.

POTTED CHEESE

FOR 4

45g/1^1/2oz butter
30g/1oz walnuts
115g/4oz Cheddar cheese
few drops of Worcestershire sauce
 (optional)
1 tbsp beer
pepper

1 Melt 20g/^{1}/2oz of the butter in a pan over a low heat.

2 Meanwhile, put the walnuts in a food processor. Whizz briefly until they are chopped quite coarsely. Add the cheese, the remaining butter and the Worcestershire sauce, if using. Whizz again briefly (be careful not to overprocess the cheese).

3 With the machine still running, slowly add the beer. As soon as it has

mixed in to form a thick paste, turn off the food processor.

4 Turn the contents out into a suitable bowl or pot and, using a spatula, pack it down firmly and then smooth over the top. Pour over the melted butter to seal it. Store in the refrigerator until required.

Variation
Use a blue cheese such as Stilton, substituting port for the beer.

SMOKED SALMON OMELETTE SOUFFLÉ

As well as making a rather elegant light and tasty breakfast or brunch dish, this is perfect for those occasions during the festivities when you yearn for a savoury snack or late supper dish but simply cannot face any more cold meats.

FOR 6

**115g/4oz smoked salmon
(trimmings will do)
5 tbsp crème fraîche
8 eggs
55g/2oz mature farmhouse
Cheddar cheese
handful of chive stalks (optional)
30g/1oz butter
30g/1oz Parmesan cheese
salt and pepper**

1 Chop the smoked salmon and mix with the crème fraîche in a large bowl. Season well (this amount will serve to season the eggs after they are added).

2 Separate the eggs, beat the yolks lightly and mix into the cream mixture, then grate in the Cheddar and mix well.

3 In a large bowl, beat the egg whites until standing in stiff peaks. Take 2 or 3 large spoonfuls of this and add to the salmon mixture. Snip in the chives, if using, and mix well to loosen the mixture. Then add the remaining egg whites and fold in lightly but thoroughly using the side of a large metal spoon.

4 Preheat a fairly hot grill, warm a flameproof serving dish (but don't let it get too hot) and melt the butter in a large heavy frying pan over a moderate heat. While the butter is melting, grate the Parmesan.

5 When the butter in the frying pan is just starting to colour, add the omelette mixture and cook over a low to moderate heat until the edges start to puff up. Shake the pan from time to time and as soon as the omelette starts to move freely around in the pan, indicating the bottom has set, slide it out on to the warmed serving dish and dust with the grated Parmesan.

6 Place under the grill and cook until well risen and golden on top. Serve immediately.

Variations

If you want to add a herb garnish, use some extra chive stalks or some flat-leaf parsley. For a grand finish, garnish with lumpfish roe or salmon eggs.

Smoked Salmon Omelette Soufflé

PARSNIP, CELERIAC AND POTATO GRATIN

Gratins usually demand long cooking. Here, shredding the vegetables and turning them in hot butter first speeds up the process considerably.

FOR 8-10

30g/1oz butter
450g/1lb parsnips
450g/1lb celeriac
450g/1lb potatoes
1 large onion
3 plump garlic cloves
115g/4oz mature farmhouse Cheddar cheese
575ml/1pt crème fraîche
large pinch of paprika
large pinch of mustard powder
salt and pepper

1 Preheat the oven to 200°C/400°F/gas 6. Use a little of the butter to grease the sides of a large heatproof casserole.

2 Peel all the vegetables except the onion and shred them, using the shredding blade of the food processor. Turn them all out on a large clean tea towel and pat and squeeze as dry as possible.

3 Put the casserole over a moderate heat on the hob and melt the remaining butter in it. Peel and chop the onion and garlic, then sauté them

briefly until just translucent. Add the shredded vegetables and turn for a minute or so to coat with butter. Remove from the heat.

4 Grate the cheese and mix half into the cream, then season it with the paprika, mustard, salt and pepper.

5 Pour the cream over the shredded vegetables and sprinkle the remaining cheese over the top.

6 Bake for about 30 minutes, until golden brown.

BRAISED RED CABBAGE WITH TANGERINES

FOR 6

450g/1lb red cabbage
1 tbsp white wine vinegar
1 tbsp groundnut or sunflower oil
45g/1½oz butter
pinch each of ground nutmeg and ground cinnamon
1 tsp sugar
2 tsp fresh orange juice
2 sweet ripe tangerines or clementines
salt and pepper

1 Cut out and discard the core of the cabbage, then shred it finely. Put the cabbage in a large sauté pan, season with a little salt and cover with cold water. Add the vinegar. Bring to a simmer, leave to cook for 5 minutes, then drain and reserve.

2 Return the pan to a moderate heat. Heat the oil and, when hot, add the butter and spices. Stir for 1 minute.

3 Tip in the cabbage, sprinkle with the sugar and orange juice and stir for 2-3 minutes.

4 Cover and leave to cook gently while you skin the tangerines and separate the segments.

5 Add the segments to the pan. Stir, then cover and cook for 2-3 minutes, shaking the pan occasionally. Season.

Braised Red Cabbage with Tangerines

CHRISTMAS CLUB SANDWICH

A club sandwich is the ideal way to use up any leftovers. It's best made with interesting bread – sourdough, wholemeal, or a good baguette.

FOR 2

4 rashers of unsmoked middle bacon
2 egg yolks
2 tbsp lemon juice
150ml/^{1}/$_4$pt olive oil
150ml/^{1}/$_4$pt sunflower oil
45g/1^1/$_2$oz Stilton cheese
2 medium tomatoes
1 tsp balsamic vinegar
^{1}/$_2$ avocado
small bunch of flat-leaf parsley
6 slices of good bread (see above)
4 slices of cooked turkey
salt and pepper

1 Grill the bacon until crisp.

2 Meanwhile, make a mayonnaise in a food processor by whizzing the egg yolks with 1 tablespoon of lemon juice. Mix the oils together and then, with the machine still running, trickle them in and process until thick and creamy. Add the Stilton and a teaspoon of lemon juice and whizz again until the cheese is well mixed in. Adjust the seasoning.

3 Slice the tomatoes and sprinkle with vinegar. Peel and slice the avocado and sprinkle with lemon juice. Chop the parsley. Cut each bacon rasher in half.

4 Spread 2 slices of bread on one side with mayonnaise and scatter over a little parsley. Put the bacon and avocado on top. Scatter over more parsley and season to taste. Spread 2 more slices of bread on both sides with the mayonnaise and lay these on top.

5 Arrange half of the tomato slices on the bread. Top with turkey, then add the remaining tomato and season. Finally, spread the remaining 2 slices of bread on one side with the mayonnaise and lay them, spread side down, on top. Secure each sandwich with an orange stick and serve.

TURKEY FRICASSÉE

FOR 3–4

2 tbsp groundnut or sunflower oil
1 garlic clove
6 tbsp port or medium sherry
1 tbsp grainy mustard
several sprigs of flat-leaf parsley
^{1}/$_2$ tsp dried thyme
^{1}/$_2$ tsp dried rubbed sage
^{1}/$_2$ small orange
few drops each of Tabasco and Worcestershire sauce
about 450g/1lb cooked turkey
2 tbsp cream
20g/^{1}/$_2$oz butter
salt and pepper

1 Heat the oil until very hot in a large wok, sauté pan or frying pan. Smash, peel and crush the garlic. Add to the pan and stir for a few seconds, then stir in the port, mustard, parsley, sage and thyme (reserve a few sprigs of parsley for garnish).

2 Grate in a little orange zest and squeeze in the juice. Add a few drops each of Tabasco and Worcestershire sauce. Simmer the mixture for 1–2 minutes, stirring frequently.

3 Cut the turkey into strips and add to the pan. Reduce the heat and cook for about 3 minutes until heated through, stirring frequently.

4 Stir in the cream and butter. Adjust the seasoning. Snip over the rest of the parsley and serve as soon as possible.

TURKEY BROTH

For this rich broth, use all the turkey bones and trimmings, including skin, you can find – dark meat, legs and thighs will give you more flavour than breast meat, so keep the breast meat for sandwiches.

leftover roast turkey plus bones, skin and other trimmings (see above)
2 bay leaves
10 black peppercorns
4-6 celery stalks, with leaves
3-4 carrots
2-3 leeks
1 large onion
handful of parsley
55g/2oz basmati rice
150ml ¼pt crème fraîche
few drops of Worcestershire sauce
salt and pepper

1 Put the turkey in a large pan with the bay leaves, peppercorns and a generous pinch of salt. Pour over water to cover and place over a high heat.

2 Rinse and trim the celery stalks, carrots and leeks. Top and tail the onion but leave the skin on. Chop it into quarters. Coarsely chop 2 of the celery stalks and 1 of the carrots. As they are ready, add the chopped onion, carrot and celery to the pan, together with the rinsed stalks from the parsley and the rinsed green trimmings from the leeks. Add more water if necessary.

3 When the contents of the pan come to a boil, leave to boil rapidly for a few minutes, then skim off any scum from the surface .

4 Leave to simmer for about 20 minutes. Meanwhile, finely chop the remaining vegetables.

5 At the end of the 20 minutes, strain the stock through a colander and return to the pan. Add the freshly chopped vegetables and rice and bring back to a simmer. Leave to simmer for about 10 minutes, or until the vegetables and rice are just tender.

6 Meanwhile, when cool enough to handle, shred any meat from the turkey trimmings and chop finely.

7 Stir the turkey into the soup with the crème fraîche. Adjust the seasoning with salt, pepper and Worcestershire sauce and snip in the parsley to finish.

CHRISTMAS PUDDING ICE CREAM

about 575ml/1pt good-quality vanilla ice cream
about 140-170g/5-6oz leftover Christmas pudding
1 generous tbsp marmalade
1 tbsp Cointreau
1-2 tbsp brandy

1 Remove the ice cream from the freezer and allow it to soften slightly.

2 Spoon or tip the pudding into a food processor and whizz for a few seconds. Scrape the pudding away from the sides of the bowl.

3 Add the ice cream, marmalade, Cointreau and brandy. Whizz briefly .

4 Transfer the mixture to a suitable container and freeze. Remove the ice cream from the freezer a few minutes before serving.

Treasury of
basic recipes
to impress
without effort

No-cook or Quick
Condiments or Dips

No-cook or Quick
Sauces

Quick Ways with
Convenience Foods

No-cook or Quick Ways
with Cream

Quick Ways with Bread

Mango Chutney Cream Dip

One or two large spoonfuls of mild and sweet mango chutney stirred into a small pot of crème fraîche makes a delicious dip for vegetable crudités or mini poppadams (some supermarkets now sell packs of assorted flavours and colours for an attractive nibbles tray).

Blue Cheese and Walnut Dip

Mash a creamy blue cheese like Gorgonzola or Pipo Crème with a little pouring cream until you reach a dipping consistency, then stir in some coarsely chopped walnut halves. Serve with crudités or strips of warmed pitta bread.

Parmesan and Red Onion Dip

Finely chop a red onion and stir into some crème fraîche. Grate in a large chunk of Parmesan and season with black pepper. Serve as a dip with vegetable crudités or small leaves of chicory and radicchio.

Aïoli

Pound 2 or 3 garlic cloves to a paste with a little sea salt in a pestle with a mortar and add this to the egg when making Blender Mayonnaise (see right). Stir in just enough lemon juice to give a dipping consistency. This is one of the nicest dips to serve with vegetable crudités, but it is also good with eggs, fish and shellfish.

Avocado Cheese Dip

Whizz the contents of a small tub of plain cottage cheese until smooth. Snip in 3 or 4 spring onions and a handful each of coriander and parsley. Season with the juice of 1 or 2 lemons or limes, a dash of Worcestershire sauce, salt and pepper. Halve, peel and stone 2 large ripe avocados and pulse into the mixture. Serve with corn chips.

Lime, Ginger and Chilli Relish

Grate a chunk of peeled fresh ginger into the juice of 2 limes. Deseed a red chilli pepper and chop it finely. Add to the juice and stir well. Crush in 1 or 2 garlic cloves. Deseed and finely chop a green pepper and stir in. Dissolve 1 teaspoonful of arrowroot in 2 tablespoons of white wine vinegar or sherry vinegar and stir in. Season with salt and pepper and add just enough sugar to get a sweet-and-sour balance. Serve as a dip with raw mange-tout peas and blanched baby sweetcorn or as a relish for shellfish.

English Garden Salsa

Dice 1 small cucumber into a bowl and snip in 3 or 4 spring onions. Juice a lemon, mix with a tablespoon of olive oil and 1 teaspoon of mustard powder and pour over the vegetables. Season with salt and pepper and stir well. Serve as a relish with hot and cold salmon and cold meats.

Carrot and Radish Relish

Grate a large chunk of mooli radish and 1 or 2 carrots. Toss in white wine vinegar to coat and leave to marinate for about 10 minutes. Serve with cold meats and rich terrines or fried fish. On a bed of leaves this also makes an interesting and simple first course.

Blender Mayonnaise

Break an egg (at room temperature) into a food processor, add a squeeze of lemon juice or white wine vinegar and half a measured 150ml/$\frac{1}{4}$pt of sunflower oil. Whizz briefly. With the machine still running, trickle in the remaining sunflower oil followed by 150ml/$\frac{1}{4}$pt extra virgin olive oil and process until thick and smooth. Season with salt and pepper and a little more lemon juice or vinegar, if necessary. (See page 139 for ways of adding more flavouring to mayonnaise).

Quick White Sauce

Melt 30g/1oz butter in a saucepan over gentle heat. Add 2 tablespoons of flour and stir until well mixed and bubbling. Cook for a minute or two until the colour darkens slightly. Gradually stir in 575ml/1pt milk (or a mixture of milk and stock if appropriate) and cook, stirring all the time, until bubbling and thickened. Season with celery salt, a pinch of nutmeg and pepper.

This simple recipe can be adapted in a number of ways. Sauté a finely chopped onion in the butter for an onion sauce. Snip in a generous handful of parsley for a parsley sauce. Grate in 50g/2oz mature farmhouse Cheddar, a dash of Worcestershire sauce and 2 teaspoons of made mustard for a cheese sauce.

Fresh Tomato Salsa

Chop 3 or 4 ripe plum tomatoes and 1 red onion. Deseed and finely chop a red chilli pepper. Combine all three in a bowl with the juice of 2 limes and snip in some coriander leaves. Serve with all manner of cold, grilled and fried meat, fish and poultry. Make the salsa even hotter with added cayenne or add chopped mango flesh or honey to sweeten according to taste and use. You can also vary the herbs added, such as replacing the coriander with basil or fresh tarragon when accompanying chicken. Salsas also make good dips with corn chips.

Maître d'Hôtel Butter

Soften 50g/2oz butter in a bowl. Snip in a handful of flat-leaf parsley and add a squeeze of lemon juice. Mash together and roll up into a cylinder in some foil. Chill and cut off discs as required. Use as a quick dressing for grilled meats and fish.

Make garlic butter to serve with steaks by blanching 3–4 garlic cloves in boiling water for a few minutes and mash these into the butter. Alternatively, snip in some chives and chervil with the parsley to make herb butter for grilled fish.

The same principle makes good sweet sauces for fruit desserts and sweet pancakes. Use unsalted butter and blend in citrus rind and juice or fruit liqueurs.

Green Peppercorn and Port Sauce

Briefly sauté 2 or 3 snipped spring onions in a little butter with a tablespoon of lightly crushed drained green peppercorns. Deglaze with a few spoonfuls of port and boil rapidly until almost all the liquid has gone, then whisk in a large knob of chilled butter. Serve with roast or grilled red meat.

Orange Mustard Sauce

Briefly sauté 2 or 3 snipped spring onions in a little butter. Deglaze with the juice of 1 large orange and stir in some Dijon mustard. Boil to reduce to a glaze, then whisk in a large knob of chilled butter. Serve with oily fish, duck or pork.

Horseradish and Rocket Cream

Mix 150ml/¼pt crème fraîche or sour cream with 1–2 tablespoons of freshly grated horseradish (now available in jars) and a handful of shredded rocket leaves. Serve with roast fish and meats. This also makes an excellent no-cook pasta sauce.

Herbed Olive Oil

Warm some extra virgin olive oil in a pan and snip in plenty of fresh herbs, such as chives, chervil, basil and tarragon. Pour over potatoes and other boiled or grilled vegetables, use as a salad dressing or pasta sauce, or even serve as a dip with good crusty bread.

Fruit Sauce

Purée some berry fruit with honey or icing sugar and a little lemon zest and juice to make the perfect sauce for creamy desserts. Add brandy or fruit liqueurs for even more flavour. If really pressed, warm some good red fruit jam and use instead of fresh fruit.

Quick Chocolate Sauce

Melt 30g/1oz unsalted butter in a small pan with 2 tablespoons of water. Break in 85g/3oz best-quality dark chocolate and stir until smooth. Stir in 2 tablespoons of thick cream. Flavour with finely chopped stem ginger or a little green ginger wine, or a little sherry or brandy — or even crème de menthe. Pour over ice cream or use as a dip with summer fruit.

QUICK WAYS WITH CONVENIENCE FOODS

Smoked Salmon Blinis

For a stylish first course or snack, lightly toast blinis (sold in packs near the smoked fish in supermarket chill counters), smear with crème fraîche and arrange slices of smoked salmon on each. Snip over some spring onion and sprinkle with lemon juice and black pepper.

Hummus

Whizz drained canned chickpeas with several garlic cloves, 3–4 tablespoons of tahini (sesame seed paste), 3–4 tablespoons of olive oil and just enough lemon juice to sharpen. Season and serve with pitta bread warmed in the toaster.

Artichoke Hearts with Goats' Cheese

Place slices of goats' cheese on top of some drained canned artichoke hearts and grill until the cheese bubbles. Serve on a bed of radicchio leaves for a first course, or with drinks.

Flavoured Mayonnaise

Cheer up bought mayonnaise with a spoonful or two of grainy mustard (for ham and oily fish), a little cream and some chopped herbs (for vegetable and egg dishes) or crushed garlic for aïoli (see page 138). Mash in the flesh of half an avocado and some lemon juice to dress a tomato salad.

No-cook Fish Pâté

Drain a can of sardines, mash together with 2–3 tablespoons of bought or Blender Mayonnaise (see page 138), 2–3 finely chopped tomatoes and a squeeze of lemon juice. Add salt, pepper and a dash each of Worcestershire sauce and Tabasco. Serve with toast and lemon wedges.

Oriental Chicken Pancakes

Stuff ready-made Oriental pancakes with shredded leftover chicken mixed with plum sauce and chopped spring onions. Heat in the microwave for a first course.

Tuna and Anchovy Paste

Whizz drained canned tuna with 3–4 drained anchovy fillets, a tablespoon of chopped drained capers, 2–3 gherkins and a little olive oil until smooth. With the machine still running, add more oil in a steady stream until you have a sauce-like consistency. Season with pepper and lemon juice and spread over cold meats.

Clam and Cream Cheese Spread

Drain a can of chopped clams and stir into some soft cream cheese with a little lemon juice, a pinch of oregano, some celery salt and a touch of cayenne pepper. Serve on crackers or thick cucumber slices with drinks or thin with cream for a dip.

Fruit and Cream Baskets

Fill bought sponge bases or chocolate shells with Crema Nostra or Screwdriver Cream (see pages 141–2) and top with fresh berries or sliced nectarines.

Prompt Pavlova

Fill a ready-made meringue shell with Rapid Romanoff (see page 141), top with some raspberries and passion fruit pulp.

Cream and good-quality plain runny yogurt are great stand-bys for the quick cook. If your refrigerator contains a large carton of whipping or double cream, crème fraîche or Greek-style yogurt, you are only minutes from some fascinating classic last courses that are filled with flavour and have the right touch of luxury to set the seal on a special meal. Fresh soft cheeses like fromage frais, ricotta or mascarpone also have the same potential and work particularly well studded with fairly solid flavourings, like fruit or nuts.

If you are worried about the healthiness of such desserts, there are now reduced-fat versions of most of these products, but remember that the fat is a fairly significant factor in the taste. Also, low-calorie sugar substitutes may be used to sweeten any of the following dishes.

GINGER POSSET

This is particularly good for cleansing the palate after a spicy meal.
For 6

about 6 pieces of stem ginger in
**   syrup**
575ml/1pt chilled double cream
6–8 tbsp ginger wine
2 tbsp whisky
icing sugar (optional)
langues de chat or Florentines,
**   to serve**

1 Chop the ginger finely and measure out about 3 tablespoons of the syrup.
2 Whip the cream to soft peaks.
3 Whisk in the ginger, ginger wine and whisky a little at a time, keeping the consistency of the cream smooth and soft at all times.
4 Sweeten to taste with icing sugar, if necessary.
5 Spoon into glasses, coupes or small bowls and chill until ready to serve.
6 Just before serving, drizzle the ginger syrup over the top. Serve with langues de chat or Florentines.

MOCK TUDOR SYLLABUB

A version of this concoction — closely related to Italian *zabaglione* — was taken as a restorative drink in Elizabethan times. It is very good after roasts.
For 4–6

whites of 2 eggs
2 tbsp caster sugar
1 lemon
4 tbsp dry sherry
2 tbsp brandy
300ml/$\frac{1}{2}$pt chilled double cream
nutmeg, to decorate (optional)
macaroons, crêpes dentelles or
**   brandy snaps, to serve**

1 In a large bowl, whisk the egg whites to stiff peaks (use the yolks for mayonnaise or to enrich sauces).
2 Fold in the sugar, the juice from the lemon, the sherry and the brandy.
3 In another bowl, whip the cream to soft peaks.
4 Fold the cream into the contents of the first bowl.
5 Spoon the mixture into sundae or tall champagne glasses and chill for as long as possible.

6 If you like, decorate with a few strips of pared lemon zest or a dusting of freshly grated nutmeg.

7 Serve with macaroons, crêpes dentelle or brandy snaps.

FAST FRUIT 'N' NUT WHIP

For 4–6

300 ml/¹/₂ pt chilled double cream
1 small lemon
85g/3oz good-quality nut brittle
50g/2oz seedless raisins

1 Whip the cream to soft peaks.

2 Grate in the zest of the lemon.

3 Crush the nut brittle into fairly small pieces (but not a powder), either in a mortar with a pestle or in a plastic bag beaten with a rolling pin or mallet. Stir into the cream with the raisins.

4 Spoon into glasses, coupes or small bowls and chill until ready to serve.

ATHOLL BROSE

This is the deluxe sweet version of the traditional country Scottish dish 'brose', made from oatmeal, butter and the cooking 'bree' from boiling the 'neeps' or turnips.

For 4–6

300ml/¹/₂pt chilled double cream
3 tbsp clear honey
4 heaped tbsp oatmeal
2 tbsp whisky
shortbread biscuits (preferably petticoat tails), to serve

1 Whip the cream until standing in soft peaks.

2 Stir in the other ingredients.

3 Spoon into glasses or bowls and chill for as long as possible before serving.

4 Serve with shortbread biscuits.

WARM CARIBBEAN BALM

For 6–8

225g/8oz canned pineapple pieces in syrup
1 tsp instant coffee granules
5 tbsp rum
575ml/1pt double cream
amaretti or ratafia biscuits, to serve

1 Tip the pineapple with 3–4 tablespoons of its syrup into a frying pan, stir in the coffee and bring to a bubble over a high heat. Continue to cook for about 5–7 minutes, until reduced and beginning to caramelize.

2 Off the heat, pour over the rum and flame carefully.

3 When the flames have died down, return to a lower heat and stir in the cream to warm through.

4 Serve immediately with amaretti or ratafia biscuits.

RAPID ROMANOFF

Use fresh fruit for the best results, but defrosted frozen berries also work well.

For 4–6

300ml/¹/₂pt chilled Greek-style yogurt
170g/6oz raspberries
icing sugar

1 Whizz all but a few of the best-looking berries very briefly in the food processor to give a chunky purée.

2 Pour the purée into a bowl, stir in the yogurt and mix well.

3 Sweeten to taste with icing sugar.

4 Spoon into bowls, coupes or glasses and chill.

5 Decorate with the reserved fruit to serve.

SCREWDRIVER CREAM

A 'screwdriver' is the name for the bracing vodka and orange juice pick-me-up which is so popular at American brunches. This orange-zest-and-vodka-flavoured cream makes a vivid accompaniment to most fresh fruit. Alternatively, try it as a topping or a filling in a ready-made sponge cake, or in chocolate shells as suggested on page 140.

For 4

300ml/¹/₂pt chilled crème fraîche
1 large orange
2–3 tbsp vodka
icing sugar, to taste
fresh fruit or biscuits, to serve

1 In a bowl, whip the crème fraîche to soft peaks.

2 Grate in the zest of the orange and stir in the vodka.

3 Sweeten to taste with icing sugar, if necessary.

4 Spoon the mixture into glasses, coupes or small bowls and chill in the refrigerator until ready to serve.

5 Serve with fresh fruit or biscuits, or use as suggested above.

CREMA NOSTRA

This is based on the wonderful Sicilian dessert *cannoli*, which consists of deep-fried pastry tubes filled with a similarly flavoured ricotta.

For 6–8

50g/2oz shelled unsalted pistachio nuts
350g/12 oz chilled ricotta cheese
85g/3oz chopped candied peel
1 tbsp orange-flower water
chocolate chip cookies, shortbread biscuits or brandy snaps, to serve

1   Coarsely chop the pistachios.

2   Put the cheese in a bowl. Stir the chopped nuts into the cheese together with the remaining ingredients.

3   Serve with chocolate chip cookies, shortbread biscuits or brandy snaps.

INSTANT TIRAMISU

For 6–8

12 sponge fingers

1 tsp instant coffee granules

2 tbsp brandy

2 tbsp Marsala

3 eggs

3 tbsp caster sugar

350g/12oz mascarpone or ricotta cheese

85g/3oz bitter chocolate

1   Tear half the sponge fingers into chunks and scatter in the bottom of a serving bowl.

2   Dissolve the coffee in 2 tablespoons of boiling water and add half the brandy and Marsala. Sprinkle half of this over the sponge pieces.

3   Separate the eggs and, in a large bowl, beat the yolks with the sugar briefly until well mixed.

4   Beat the cheese into the egg yolk mixture a little at a time until it has all been incorporated. Beat in the remaining tablespoon each of brandy and Marsala.

5   Whisk the egg whites until stiff and fold into the cheese mixture.

6   Coarsely grate one-third of the chocolate over the sponge layer and then spoon half the cheese mixture over it.

7   Repeat the sponge, coffee mixture and cheese mixture layers again. Grate the remaining chocolate over the top and chill in the refrigerator for as long as possible before serving.

QUICK WAYS WITH BREAD

Garlic Croutons

Remove the crusts from some thickly sliced white bread and cut into cubes. Rub the insides of a frying pan well with garlic, melt some butter in it and sauté the bread cubes until golden. Serve sprinkled in soups (like the Chowder on page 51) or use to add texture to salads and egg dishes.

Croûtes

Make croûtes as bases on which to serve egg dishes or roast poultry by cutting thick slices of stale bread either in squares or triangles (or in rounds with a pastry cutter) and frying in butter until golden.

Bread Salads

For a salad akin to Middle-eastern fattoush and Mediterranean panzanella, toast stale bread, break up into pieces and toss in a mustardy salad dressing, then add chopped tomatoes and cucumber and snipped spring onions and herbs, such as coriander and mint.

Pain Perdu

Dip slices of bread or brioche in a sweetened egg batter and fry in unsalted butter. Add cinnamon or orange zest to the batter if you like, and dust the cooked toast with icing sugar. This works well as a base for good-quality ice cream.

Bruschetta

Brush thick toasted slices of crusty bread with extra virgin olive oil, smear with a cut garlic clove and add a topping such as chopped tomatoes, olives, anchovies and Mozzarella. Grill again briefly if necessary.

Marmite Soldiers

Grill slices of white bread on one side only and spread the untoasted sides with butter and Marmite. Grill this side for a minute or so. Cut into strips, these icons of childhood make smart accompaniments to egg and cheese dishes.

Brie Toasts

Arrange some wedges of Brie on thick slices of brioche spread lightly with Dijon mustard and toast until the cheese bubbles. Serve as a first course or with drinks. If you have time, sprinkle with toasted almonds.

Fruit Croissants

For an unusual breakfast or dessert, warm some croissants, split open and fill with fresh berries tossed in sweetened cream.

Quick Summer Charlotte

Line a dish with slices of buttered crustless brown bread or brioche and fill with Warm Caribbean Balm (see page 141) or spread with warmed apple sauce and fill with Rapid Romanoff (page 141).

Instant Bread and Butter Pudding

Butter some trimmed slices of stale bread, brioche or cake and layer in a dish with sultanas soaked in orange juice or brandy. Pour over some made-up packet custard, leave to cool slightly and let the custard soak into the bread. If you like, flavour the bread layers with marmalade.